Praise for *The Way Between*

"This novel should be read aloud to everyone, by everyone, from childhood onward. Rivera Sun writes in a style as magical as Tolkien and as authentic as Twain." - Tom Hastings, Director of PeaceVoice, Professor of Conflict Studies at Portland State University

"Rivera Sun has, once again, used her passion for nonviolence and her talent for putting thoughts into powerful words on a page to recreate life and to show us the possibilities that can be, if we dedicate ourselves to *The Way Between*." -Robin Wildman, Fifth Grade Teacher, Nonviolent Schools Movement, and Nonviolence Trainer

"A wonderful book! It is so rare to find exciting fiction for young people and adults that shows creative solutions to conflict, and challenges violence with active nonviolence and peace. Ari Ara is a delightful character and this story is a gem." - Heart Phoenix, River Phoenix Center for Peacebuilding

"A beautiful story that expands the imagination into the possibilities of peace and active nonviolence . . . this book will prepare our children and ourselves for the real-life world we so desperately need." - David Hartsough, Founder Nonviolent Peaceforce, author of Waging Peace

"I love the book! It's a great adventure tale, with all the elements of a classic legend, and an even more important message. " - Michael Colvin, Fellowship of Reconciliation, National Council Member

The Way Between is a compelling and wise articulation of the human sojourn . . . a dispatch from a mythic dimension of archaic longing and potential that calls us to our truest selves." - Ken Butigan, Pace e Bene/Campaign Nonviolence, Peace and Justice Studies Professor at DePaul University

The Way Between

The Way Between

Copyright © 2016 by Rivera Sun

Rising Sun Press Works
P.O. Box 1751, El Prado, NM 87529
www.riverasun.com

Library of Congress Control Number:
2016958392

ISBN 978-0-9966391-3-2 (paperback)
978-1-948016-97-1 (hardback)
978-0-9966391-5-6 (ebook)
Sun, Rivera 1982-
The Way Between

*For my friends in the peace movement
and Veterans for Peace
and also to all the young people
yearning to follow the Way Between.*

Other Works
by Rivera Sun

Novels, Books & Poetry
The Lost Heir
The Dandelion Insurrection
The Roots of Resistance
Billionaire Buddha
Steam Drills, Treadmills, and Shooting Stars
Rebel Son
Skylandia: Farm Poetry From Maine
The Dandelion Insurrection Study Guide
Freedom Stories: volume one
The Imagine-a-nation of Lala Child

RISING SUN
PRESS WORKS

A Community Published Book Supported By

Gloria Sirrine Switzer
Ken Butigan
Cindy Reinhardt
Catherine E Breheny
Elizabeth McGauley Sarfaty
Robert Simonds and Leslie Cottrell Simonds
Maja Bengtson
Bruce and Elly Nygren
January Sadler
Marirose NightSong & Daniel Podgurski
Michael Colvin, Fellowship of Reconciliation,
National Council Member
Burt Kempner
Adam, Dolly, Wyatt, Austyn and Xyler Vogal
Sunshine Jones
Jaige Trudel
Susan Carroll
Colleen Mills, Citizens for Peace President
Nancy Audette
Pamela Twining
Brian Cummings
Jean Buchanan
Casey Dorman
Carol and Romaldo Ranellone
David J. Spofford
Paul Stein, Ph.D
Rob Garvey
Hilda J Richey
Galynne & Mark Riggenbach
Moriah Hope Musick
Lynn and Chris Wadelton
John Mazzola
Sister Mary Pendergast, RSM
Patricia, Leo and Eva Charbonneau
Amanda Mehl West

Ellen Friedman
Robin Farrin, Community Activist
Stefania Tomaskovic
Jen Respass
Lynne A. Dews
Stephanie N. Van Hook
Judith Detert-Moriarty
Valerie J Deur
Rene Jalbert
Nanci Gosling Blackmarr
Carol Jussaume, RSM
DeLores H. Cook
Gail and Ken Kailing
Deanna Ross
SuRu
Erin Sanborn
Beverly Campbell
Rosalie Riegle
Rebekkah Hilgraves
Heart Phoenix, River Phoenix Center for Peacebuilding
Molly Gordon, Master Certified Coach
JoAnn Bennie Huber
Christine Upton
Crystal Marie Ramos Saldana
Cindy Barnes
Clifford and Lesley Scott

Thank you!

The Way Between

by
Rivera Sun

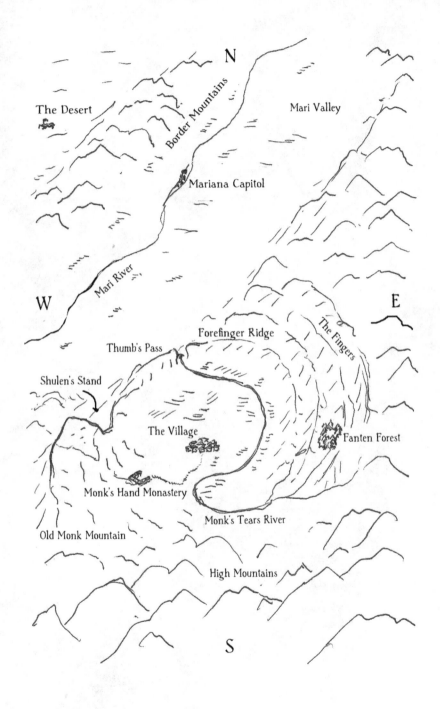

N

The Desert

Border Mountains

Mari Valley

Mariana Capitol

Mari River

W   E

Forefinger Ridge

The Fingers

Thumb's Pass

Shulen's Stand

The Village

Fanten Forest

Monk's Hand Monastery

Monk's Tears River

Old Monk Mountain

High Mountains

S

CHAPTER ONE

. . . . .

The Horns of Monk's Hand bellowed low and sonorous. Ari Ara skidded to a halt. As the deep tones rolled around the echoing bowl of the valley, the girl's blue-grey eyes traced the sound back to the stone-carved monastery far below. The Horns announced the change of seasons. Autumn had arrived.

She leapt across the black rocks of the High Mountains. The wind flung back the hood of her thick, black wool shepherdess cloak. Her red hair burned bright against the steep slopes. The sky blazed cold blue. The wind nearly knocked her off her feet.

As she hurtled down the outcropping, she put her fingers in her mouth and whistled. Sharp and distinctive, the tone shrilled high then low. It was a Fanten call, one that echoed through the forests below on dark nights before moonrise. In the meadow, the tall black-fleeced Fanten sheep lifted their heads.

Autumn! Ari Ara leapt off the ledge and landed in a crouch. She shivered, glancing up at the ferocious blue sky. Cold gripped the air on the higher ridges. The silver mists hinted of snow. Ari Ara jogged toward the high altitude meadow where her flock grazed. She had the build of a shepherdess - wiry and

1

strong, muscles tight to bones, eyes that scanned the distances, and a sense of the wide sky in her stance. Her cheeks reddened with the cold, skin already roughened by the harsh winds of the High Mountains. A pair of worn, ragged boots bound her legs up to her knees. Her breeches vanished beneath a tunic. On top, she wore a shepherdess cloak felted tight enough to keep out the rain and snow.

Again, the Horns sounded, calling the farmers in from the harvest. Ari Ara raced around a tumble of rocks into the golden grasses and skidded to a stop among the sheep. The lead ewe flicked her ears at the girl and trotted over. Ari Ara stretched out her hand in greeting. The warm breath of the sheep's muzzle tickled her palm. The wind chilled it quickly. Like all Fanten sheep, the long-legged ewe stood nearly four feet tall at her back. She was old; her fleece had silvered nearly to white. The days of her coal-black youth had long passed, but the strands of her fleece still stretched the length of Ari Ara's arm. Fanten sheep were considered the finest in all of Mariana, but they would only live in the High Mountains, not in the lowlands down by Mari River and the Capital. Rumors claimed that the uncanny black sheep followed only Fanten shepherdesses, but Ari Ara knew it was familiarity and trust - not the scent of the Fanten in her blood - that brought the sheep to her.

She was an orphan. No one knew her parentage and no one cared. No one - Fanten, monk, or villager - claimed her as one of their kind. *Ari Ara*, she was named, *not this, not that*. A child who belonged to no one, but roamed the wide bowl of the crater valley, the deep forests, and the High Mountains on her own. Shaped like the fingers of a meditating monk, the Monk's Hand Mountains loomed dark, mysterious, and serene. The villagers' fields and houses nestled in the broad, flat palm. The

Thumb's Pass met the Forefinger Ridge in a narrow opening where the river rushed down into Mari Valley. The Fanten Forest covered the sharp, forbidding slopes of the three Fingers - a series of deep ravines carved by rivers, wind, and time. This rugged landscape formed the outer range of her world. It took a full day to cross the crater valley and years to explore the looming mountains. Ari Ara knew the High Mountains well from her time watching the Fanten flock. Monk's Hand had grown as familiar as her own.

"Autumn has arrived," Ari Ara told the ewe, nodding to the peaks as the Horns of Monk's Hand Monastery thundered again. "It's time to go down the mountain."

The mother bleated. The flock echoed the call. Ari Ara spun and took off at a run. She did not look back. Once the lead ewe understood, the flock would always follow. The girl leapt over the boulders and the sheep flowed behind her.

At the crossroads, they turned onto the narrow path to the right, snaking down toward the shelter of the Fanten Forest. Massive trees towered overhead, anchored with a web of connected roots that ran vast distances beneath the earth. Under the boughs, the air hung cool and still. The thud of the sheep's hooves fell muffled as they trotted along the thick carpet of needles. With their black, shining wool, the sheep slid through the dark shadowed wood, nearly invisible.

The silver-haired Fanten Grandmother, headwoman of the group, stood waiting in the inner grove. Ari Ara halted, chest heaving and cheeks burning with warmth. You could never sneak up on a Fanten . . . though they startled everyone else with their secretive ways, silent footsteps, and sudden appearances. In the carved caves under the bases of the trees, the Fanten lived warm and protected.

"Well, now," the old woman spoke in her own tongue, greeting the mother ewe. "How did she care for you this summer?"

The little woman stood just barely taller than Ari Ara. Her silver-white Fanten cloak came from the mother ewe's back. The ewe laid her muzzle in the cupped hands of the grandmother. They studied each other in a long and silent exchange.

Ari Ara waited for the verdict, thinking back over the season. She remembered how a late snowstorm caught them in the upper meadows, how she brought the flock to shelter, how she struggled all night to help a pair of tangled twin lambs into the world, how a wolf pack snatched one of them away and would have taken more if Ari Ara had not raced like a howling red-haired demon into their midst, hurling stones and sticks.

"Good," spoke the Fanten Grandmother. She released the mother's muzzle and stretched her wrinkled hand toward the girl.

"You've grown," she commented, her dark eyes scanning the girl. "You're tall compared to the Fanten daughters, though still short by Marianan standards. You've been like that since the beginning."

Ari Ara looked up, hopeful. Perhaps the elder would share more of her past - something more than: *you were left here as an infant. We cared for you until you were old enough to watch the sheep. Then we sent you into the mountains with the flock.*

The sheep choose the shepherd, and to the Fanten's surprise, the mother ewe picked the flame-haired Ari Ara. The village boys teased her about having a sheep for a mother - but only when she descended from the High Mountains. Otherwise, they steered clear of the Fanten sheep and the wild

4

shepherdess. The villagers' white sheep liked thicker fields. The black Fanten flocks preferred silence, solitude, and space.

"What will you do this winter, child?" the elder asked.

"I could stay here and learn the sacred dances," Ari Ara suggested hopefully.

The intricate dances of the Fanten fascinated her. She'd grown up watching the women, even learning the common ones that all the young Fanten daughters knew. But last year, Fanten Grandmother had put a stop to that, saying that Ari Ara was not one of them and had to seek her own path.

Today, the Fanten Grandmother's eyes clouded and her mouth turned down at the corners.

"It is not your fate to follow the Fanten path."

Ari Ara scowled and cursed fate. Who gave that the final say? Not her. She kicked sullenly at the ground.

"Maybe I'll just go back into the mountains and live in a cave," she grumbled.

"Don't be ridiculous," the Fanten Grandmother snapped. "Go to the village like you did last year."

"I can't," she muttered, scuffing the needles on the ground with her heel. "The village leader threw me out midwinter for causing trouble."

"And did you?" the wrinkled old woman demanded.

"Not half as much as I wanted to," Ari Ara admitted fiercely.

The elder hid a smile.

"You ought to learn to read and write," she told her.

Ari Ara made a face.

"What good is book learning to a shepherdess?" she complained.

"You won't be a shepherdess forever."

The Fanten Grandmother's voice rang prophetically, snapping Ari Ara out of her sulking. She stared at the old woman who stood silver and white against the black shadows of the trees. The elder's dark eyes gazed at the swaying boughs. The wind whispered secrets in the glossy needles. She tilted her head as if listening. Ari Ara's blue-grey eyes lifted, but she saw only the outlines of branches against the sky beyond. She sensed, as she always did, that the mysterious Fanten knew far more than they revealed.

The Fanten Grandmother dropped her gaze to the girl. She sighed. That child was always pushing fate . . . and it would get her into trouble one day.

"Go to the village and apologize to the leader," she told the girl firmly.

Ari Ara sighed and didn't reply.

Swiftly, before the girl asked any more questions, the old Fanten bent, kissed the crown of the girl's bright red hair and said the ritual words, "Thank you for keeping our flock safe. We honor you for that gift."

Ari Ara accepted the ritual words moodily.

The delicate old woman pursed her lips and sounded her whistle. She turned into the forest; the mother ewe and flock followed. Ari Ara stared after her for a moment, then spun on her heel and ran off in the other direction. Hearing her soft footsteps departing, the Fanten Grandmother paused. Her eyes widened, remembering.

"Ari Ara!" she called.

But it was too late. The flame of her hair vanished.

The child was gone.

CHAPTER TWO

. . . . .

The Horns shook the rocks as she raced out of the Fanten Forest and across the lower meadows. At the crossroads, Ari Ara halted and stood defiantly in the buffeting wind. The trail down to the village stretched out, wide and predictable. She cast a glance up toward the black peaks of the High Mountains. She had spent the second half of last winter up there . . . but the deep snows nearly froze her at night - and that was after the coldest months had already passed. She turned reluctantly to look at the village. The thatched roofs huddled together like a cluster of haystack sheep. The villagers spent cramped winters inside, bickering and teasing each other. She made a face. She would *not* go to the village and apologize. It wasn't her fault - not all of it. The very idea of asking for forgiveness rankled her. She'd rather winter in the mountains.

The Horns of Monk's Hand roared again. Ari Ara pivoted toward the sound. A laugh leapt out of her throat and echoed off the black rocks. She wouldn't go to the village. She'd go to the monastery! If it was a choice between a cold winter in the mountains or humiliation in the village, she chose neither! Wasn't that her name? Ari Ara. *Not this. Not that.*

Ari Ara shifted her fate in a single determined stride. She ran over the rough stones of the boulder slide. A thrill tingled in her blood. The monastery was not forbidden, not exactly, but the Fanten disapproved of the warrior monks and their endless preparations for battle. Ari Ara had been told to steer clear of them. She shivered with rebellious anticipation and increased her pace as she hurtled down the series of switchbacks that carved across the jagged slope.

She leapt onto the carved steps that stretched from the village all the way up to the monastery. The ancient buildings at the top crouched low to the ground, chiseled out of the mountainside and rumored to stretch deep into the rock behind the tiled roofs. Ari Ara remembered sneaking in once, years ago, only to be chased out by the monks. It was a place of severe angles and rambunctious orphans, serene meditations and fierce fighters. Monk's Hand Monastery brimmed with fascinating contradictions . . . but Ari Ara was determined to carve out a spot for the winter. *That would show the Fanten Grandmother,* she thought. Ari Ara climbed the stone steps two at a time, chuckling delightedly.

The Horns rumbled in her bones as twilight fell. She threw back her cloak as she reached the top, hot but barely winded. The steps were nothing compared to a lifetime of scaling the High Mountain slopes.

Minli, the one-legged orphan she'd met once in the village, was standing at the top. He was a slight boy with dark brown hair that stuck out in several directions, looking like a bird's nest atop his thin neck. The cuff of one leg of his pants was tied in a knot where his knee should have been. He had lost his limb from a sword's blow before he could even walk, one of the villagers had told her in a hushed tone. Someone had bundled him up and left him on the stone steps of the monastery in the dead of night, his leg gone, but skillfully healed. Most likely by the Fanten, the villager had speculated.

Unlike the other orphans who had been sent up from the overcrowded orphanages in Mari Valley and were originally from the Border Mountains, Minli was considered one of two Monk's Hand orphans - Ari Ara being the other. She felt an odd kinship with the one-legged boy and had made small gestures of friendship whenever their paths crossed. Neither knew who their parents were or where they had come from before appearing in the crater valley. They were simply considered part of Monk's Hand, along with craggy mountains and sweeping mists.

"Look who showed up for the autumn feast," he said, grinning.

Behind him, the monastery bustled with motion. Grey-robed warrior monks scurried across the three-sided courtyard. Small orphans shrieked with excitement and bounded in all directions. Dusk deepened over the shoulder of Old Monk Mountain, the looming giant peak that rose high above the monastery. Lights had already been lit inside. Ari Ara sniffed the air.

"Are they baking bread?" she asked.

"Yes, and sweet rolls."

"It's the bread I like best!" she enthused. The Fanten made nothing like it. During the summer season, she fared on porridge boiled from High Mountain grain. She reached out and ruffled the loose ends of his cropped hair. "How goes it, you old monk?"

"I'm not a monk and I'm not old . . . and you should be nice to me," he advised her smugly.

"Why's that?"

"There's a visitor."

"Who?" she asked, immediately curious.

"That's why you ought to be nice to me," Minli teased.

"Pfft, there's a hundred monks who'd tell me," she shrugged, but when he said nothing, she cajoled him, "I'll give you my next sweet roll if you tell me now."

"Shulen."

Ari Ara's eyes widened and she nearly toppled down the steps.

"No!" she exclaimed, craning her neck to see if she could spot the man.

Shulen was the greatest warrior on record in a thousand years. He had been the First Guard of Queen Elsinore, and then to her daughter, Queen Alinore. He had commanded the War of Retribution against the Desert People after Queen Alinore's death. In the Capital, he trained the nation's fiercest fighters. Now he was here at Monk's Hand!

"He's searching for candidates for the Guard. Rumor says that Shulen is looking to train up another Emir Miresh."

Ari Ara whistled. Emir Miresh was a legend across Mariana . . . and he hadn't even grown facial hair. He had been chosen as Shulen's apprentice at age eight and had swept the Trials every year since he was ten. No warrior stood a chance against him - except Shulen.

"So, they're searching for Guards. Any likely candidates?" Ari Ara mused.

Minli shrugged.

"Who knows? He might have simply come here because we have so many orphans. You know how the saying goes . . . "

"Good soldiers make orphans," she quoted.

"And orphans make good soldiers," Minli finished.

Ari Ara shivered at the saying. The villagers muttered it in tones that promised revenge against the Desert People for the numbers of Marianan orphans that poured out of the Border Mountains. They didn't seem to consider that the saying rang true for both sides of the conflict, and the Desert People had orphans that they might be training into soldiers, too.

Mariana and the Desert People had been fighting since the dawn of time. For a brief moment, when Queen Alinore fell in love with Tahkan Shirar, the Desert King, there was a shocked and wild hope of peace. People spoke of that time with a tone of wistful yearning . . . and an acrid bitterness for its loss. Those times sang of prophecy and legend. The coming of a golden age was on the tip of everyone's tongue, but then, swift as a thunderstorm over the mountains, their hopes were dashed. Power-hungry factions - no one knew whose - attacked the Queen, stole the Heir to both thrones (or so it was said), and vanished. The Queen died and for over a decade, violence had reigned, each side blaming the other for the Lost Heir and the dead Queen. The western border was littered with orphans, and many of them were sent to Monk's Hand Monastery to be trained into fighters.

"So, when are the Trials?" Ari Ara asked, certain that Shulen would test the trainees.

"Tonight."

"Before or after supper?" she asked, more interested in bread than fighting.

"Soon. Let's grab you a bowl of soup and bread. You can eat while we watch."

Minli hobbled quickly on his single crutch. One shoulder bunched up higher than the other, reminding her of a small crow she had once found with its claw caught in a twist of string. His black orphan's tunic flapped loosely at the sides, several sizes too large. Ari Ara followed behind him as they threaded through the brimming crowd. Spectators had already packed under the overhangs that ran along the sides of the rectangular sand-filled courtyard. No one paid attention to Ari Ara in the commotion.

Inside the kitchen, the kitchen monks chopped and argued. The two head cooks were an unlikely pair. One was thin as a broom handle and twice as knobby; Ari Ara secretly nicknamed him Nobstick. The other was round as a kettle with a shiny bald head. Teapot Monk - as Ari Ara irreverently decided to call him - hollered at them as he barreled through with a tray of sweet rolls ready for the oven.

Ari Ara closed her eyes. If there was a heaven, she imagined it to be the monks' kitchen with all its chaos and glorious smells, mouth-watering dishes and steaming heat. She could boil porridge, crack nuts, and scrounge for apples, berries and herbs in the High Mountains, but the arts of the kitchen were sheer miracles to her. Minli thrust a spoon in her hand and slopped a bowl of soup into the other. He snatched up a small loaf of bread, then nudged Ari Ara out of the kitchen before they were caught.

"Hold on," he warned her.

The last bellow of the Horns accompanied the final streak of the sunset. The monks, blowing through the huge carved instruments that stretched the entire length of the buildings, made the droning sound reverberate on and on. Ari Ara's soup rippled in the bowl and spilled over the edges. Her marrow rattled inside her bones.

When they stopped, the darkness and silence were absolute. Then she heard a flurry of rustling as the senior monks settled into cross-legged positions along the three sides of the courtyard. A torch flared and the carved face of Shulen illuminated in the gateway of the monastery.

"Are there any warriors here?"

His voice rang out in the old ritual challenge of the Trials, carrying with it echoes of all warriors since time immemorial.

Around the courtyard, the monks lifted torches into the holders on the stone pillars that held up the tiled overhang roofs. The younger monks stepped forward, along with all the trainees, and some of the boldest orphans. Ari Ara scanned their faces curiously as she licked the spilled soup from her fingers. She knew a few of the boys by sight. The rest were unfamiliar, as were the two girls who stood in the line. One of the monks dragged a tiny little boy back under the overhang. Ari Ara grinned. Usually the orphans were sent to apprentice in various trades when they reached ten years of age; that eager lad would undoubtedly be kept at Monk's Hand to train as a warrior.

Minli pointed out the ones who had come up from the Capital hoping to qualify for the coveted training positions at Monk's Hand Monastery. They ranged in age, the younger ones wishing to join the entry-level cohort, and the older youths seeking to join the intense trainings of the warrior monks.

A monk shifted his position and blocked her view.

"Psst!" Minli hissed. "Up here."

He had hopped up onto the open window of an inside room. The wide stone ledge provided just enough space to perch upon. She passed her soup and spoon up to him then jumped up in one fluid motion, twisting in midair as she did on the large boulders in the High Mountains. Minli returned the soup, spoon, and bread. They fell silent as the Trials began.

The first round was for the beginners. Ari Ara watched with only half an eye. The warm, flaky bread occupied most of her attention. Minli nudged her to watch. The older warrior monks - the ones that ran the trainings and drills - surrounded the hopeful youths. Each carried some humorous or unusual object in his hands: a plate, a wooden sled, a woven basket, one of the kitchen monks' enormous stew pots, a mattress cot, even a rolled up carpet. They brandished them at the trainees who ducked and dodged. The oldest monk leapt into action with a feather duster and a ferocity that soon had the trainees backpeddling. While the onlookers laughed, Ari Ara quickly noticed that the older monks weren't just fooling around with those objects; they were rapidly encircling the trainees, trapping them inside a solid ring.

"Those knuckleheads better break out soon or they'll be caught," she muttered as she slurped her soup.

Two of the boys and both girls broke through. The rest were caught - except for one audacious boy who leapt into the stewpot and then over the monk's startled head. Everyone cheered for that one. A gong sounded. The monks broke apart, bowing and brandishing their implements. Scores were assessed and recorded for each participant. Highest marks went to the five who had broken free.

"Now the ruckus," Minli informed her in a whisper just as a storm of movement broke out. Unarmed monks and trainees wheeled around each other in a bewildering whirlwind.

"See the poles with red scarves?" Minli explained, murmuring in her ear. "They're supposed to capture one of those scarves while the warrior monks try to block them. There's one white scarf, too. The match ends as soon as someone snags that white one. Anyone not holding a red scarf gets points taken off their score."

Ari Ara quickly sat up and scanned the poles for the white scarf.

"It's not there," she grumbled.

"It doesn't have to be on a pole," he clarified. "Sometimes it's on a belt or tied around a leg or arm."

Ari Ara searched again. She blocked out all the other sights and sounds. She narrowed her vision to find the white scarf . . . just like searching for a lost lamb on a distant hillside. A sudden flash of motion caught her eye.

"There!" she cried, elbowing Minli. "Shulen's got it. Look at him!"

Ari Ara had never seen such a sight. Shulen moved like water, grace and strength pouring off his every gesture. The white scarf was audaciously tied around his head, but no one seemed to notice him. He prowled tiger-like through the ruckus then stood stock still in the center of the courtyard. It was the hush of the spectators that alerted the trainees. They turned on Shulen, chasing him here and there.

Why were they moving as if stuck in honey? Ari Ara wondered. Then she rubbed her eyes. It was simply that Shulen moved so fast! Her mouth fell open. The ruckus continued. One red flag after another was snatched from the poles. Shulen stayed several steps ahead of even the fastest trainees. When the last red flag was pulled down, he leapt backward and held the white scarf aloft. The gong sounded.

"No one was ever going to catch him!" Ari Ara commented in an awed voice. He was a tiger playing with butterflies.

The monk in front of them turned around with a scowl and motioned for them to be silent. In the courtyard, pairs were squaring off for sparring matches. The applicants were paired according to skill levels and would work their way up in rank, moving from challenger to challenger. Ari Ara and Minli watched, whispering to each other and betting on the winners. Neither child had coins, but each carried the obligatory pocketful of polished river stones that all the young people collected. By the second stage of the matches, Minli had acquired most of hers.

"How do you know?" she complained in disgust.

"I watch them practicing," Minli explained. "I know who's steady or clever or fast or just plain strong."

"Who's the best?" she asked him.

"Of the trainees? Brol, probably," Minli answered, pointing to a powerful, dark-haired boy who had just heaved his opponent off his feet. "He's already training with the younger warrior monks."

Ari Ara shivered slightly as Brol beat his challenger back with ferocity that made her uneasy. She began to watch everyone more carefully, noting the foolish mistakes and stupid moves. *Everyone is an expert from the sidelines*, Ari Ara thought, grinning at her own impudence in critiquing the warriors-in-training.

"You ought to train," Minli suggested. "I can't, not with my leg, but you're quick and strong."

"And get whacked in the head? No, thanks," Ari Ara objected with a frown.

They flinched as a trainee took a painful blow and one of the girls swept her opponent off his feet with a swift kick.

"I'm interested in dodging blows," Ari Ara stated, "hopefully by a mile or more."

The sparring rounds made her increasingly queasy as long wooden poles replaced unarmed fighting, spears followed poles, and sword duels brought the individual trials to a climax. There were other weapons that the monks trained with, Minli informed her, but they would not be using them tonight. Ari Ara winced, watching a close shave with the sharp edge of a sword. No one was clumsy enough to be seriously hurt this evening, but Minli told her about other times when people had received painful injuries.

"Has anyone ever died?" she asked.

16

"Not recently," he answered in such a somber tone that she decided to stop asking questions.

Soon, the closing gong sounded and the sparring pairs exchanged ritual handshakes and salutes. The aroma of sweet rolls wafted as the roster of scores was carefully compiled. She saw Brol standing with the other trainees, looking pleased. He had done very well in the sparring matches and stood a good chance of receiving the highest score of the Trials.

Ari Ara leaned forward precariously as a monk walked by with a tray of sweet rolls held aloft over his shoulder. She snagged one as Minli hauled back on her belt to keep her from falling over.

"Here," she said, handing it to him and keeping her earlier bargain.

He offered her half, but she shook her head, taking another bite of the small loaf of bread. The roster of accepted trainees for this year's session at Monk's Hand was announced.

"No surprises there," Minli commented.

Most had passed, including the two girls. There were few women warriors, Minli informed Ari Ara when she asked, but they did exist. In the Capital, there was a women's cohort who were ranked at the highest levels. The two girls who passed today would likely study for a few years at Monk's Hand, then go to the Capital to complete their training as apprentices of the warrior women. Only three applicants failed the Trials: a very small orphan who could stand again next year and two youths who shrugged amiably at the news.

"They received word last week that they could apprentice to the tanners in Mari Valley," Minli told her. "They only stood Trial because they said they would. Neither showed much aptitude."

Shulen stepped calmly to the center of the courtyard.

The craggy, weathered warrior wore his iron-grey hair long, tied at the nape of his neck. His face bore more scars and crevasses than the rocky mountain slopes. The deep folds of his eyes were lined with wrinkles carved less by age than by his relentless battling with the world. He was as dark as the forest, half-shadowed in secrets, skin tanned to a gleaming shade of old bronze. He turned to the Head Monk.

"Perhaps it is time for the announcement?"

"Yes, of course," Head Monk said with a respectful bow.

A quiver of excitement ran through the crowd. The Head Monk smiled genially at them. He was a round and comfortable man who no longer trained with the warriors, though his battered nose attested to his past. A slight limp plagued him on damp days and he now preferred the warmth of a fire rather than the heat of a battle; but he was respected among the warrior monks, kind to the orphans, and skilled at managing the complex details of the monastery.

"It is our honor," he said, "to welcome the Great Warrior Shulen who will be in residence at Monk's Hand Monastery this entire year, training monks and students of all levels, and preparing the most dedicated to enter the Guard."

The crowd gasped and broke out in excited chatter.

"Unbelievable!" Minli exclaimed. "The Stone One? Here?"

"The who?" Ari Ara asked.

"The Stone One - that's what they call Shulen down in Mariana Capital."

It was an apt nickname. The hardened man had a carved quality to his presence, almost as if he had been chiseled out of the mountainside. He looked like an ancient statue awakened by magic. He neither smiled nor frowned, simply stood in the center of the courtyard with an infinite patience, waiting for the noise to die down.

Head Monk waved his hands for silence. Gradually, reluctantly, the monks, orphans, and trainees calmed.

"Let this be an inspiration to all," Head Monk said. "Hopefully, you will listen to your teachers better this year, and perhaps certain students will stop avoiding the drills that give them the strength to follow such an honored path as that of the warrior."

He shot a pointed look toward a pack of young trainees. From the darkness, a student groaned. The gathering laughed.

"Now," Head Monk continued, "it is time to honor our little orphans. Tonight, as by tradition, some will be moving into the trainees' wing to begin their paths as warriors-in-training. Others will be leaving tomorrow to start new lives in apprenticeships. Many of the ten-year-old girls will journey to the Sisters in Mari Valley to finish their upbringing with those gentle exemplars of modesty and charity. It is a night to celebrate a great many changes. Would all the orphans come forward?"

The crowd stirred as the shortest heads squeezed through to the front. Ari Ara offered Minli assistance down from the ledge then gripped his elbow.

"You're not leaving, are you?" she asked.

"No worries, there," he assured her confidently. "I'm the best scribe they've got! I'll be at Monk's Hand until I'm older than Shulen."

She breathed a sigh of relief and let him go. He made his way out into the courtyard and lined up next to the others. She peered curiously at the young people her own age, wondering at how different their lives had been. The girls had never chased wolves away from the flocks, she guessed, just as Ari Ara couldn't imagine being sent away from Monk's Hand to study with the Sisters. She shuddered at the thought.

Head Monk spoke to each in turn, assigning their new positions, gently teasing the more mischievous ones. The boys went first, followed by the girls who had been assigned to apprenticeships. Lastly, he stood before the girls who were to be sent to the Sisters, reflecting for a moment.

"Hang on," called the monk in front of Ari Ara. "You've forgotten one!"

He spun and plucked her from the ledge.

"What! No - you can't - I'm not -" she bellowed furiously.

"Not an orphan?" the monk laughed, hauling her onto the courtyard.

"Yes, I'm an orphan, but I'm not *your* orphan." She twisted in his hands, slid through his grip, and wrenched free.

"Catch her!" someone called.

Ari Ara dove to the side as the monks lunged. She rolled across the sands of the training area and leapt back to her feet just in time to spring away. Someone snatched at her cloak and she spun, throwing the end over his eyes in a trick she used on the sheep, blinding him until he let go. She whipped away. A warrior monk tried to grab hold of her - she dove head first through his wide-legged stance. As she scrambled to her feet, a trainee snatched her belt from behind and hauled her backwards. She tensed against his weight, digging her toes into the sands, then unexpectedly released, sending him flying onto his bottom. She rolled out of the tumble. She darted left . . . then right. A pair of trainees collided. A few spectators cheered her on. Someone dove for her legs; she leapt over his head. She dodged another. A circle formed around her. She imitated the little boy in the Trials and took a running leap to spring off a startled monk's shoulder out to the other side. Ari Ara whirled, not thinking, just moving, looking for an escape.

"Enough."

Shulen's voice cut through the noise like a gong. The monks and trainees froze. Ari Ara leapt at her chance. Shulen calmly caught her by the arm.

"Don't," he advised as she tried to break free.

He regarded her with an odd expression that bordered on a smile.

"Who might you be?" he demanded.

"Ari Ara," she answered hotly.

"Is that a name?" he asked, incredulous. "*Not this, not that?*"

She glared at him and didn't answer.

"And you say you're not an orphan?" he asked.

"No," she corrected. "I said that I'm not *their* orphan. I don't belong to Monk's Hand Monastery and they can't send me to the Sisters."

Shulen stroked his chin thoughtfully.

"Whom do you belong to, then?"

"No one," she answered, boldly and truthfully. She tossed her wild red hair out of her eyes. "I belong to myself . . . and only I tell myself where to go."

"Indeed," Shulen commented, raising an eyebrow. "And why didn't you show up for Trials?"

"I'm a Fanten shepherdess," she answered indignantly, "not a solider."

Shulen's face grew stern.

"There are no soldiers here. Only warriors."

"What's the difference?" she spat out with an irate shrug. "They both make wars and orphans."

The monks cried out angrily at her words. Shulen held his hand up for silence.

"A soldier is hired by the nobles and battles for their causes. A warrior takes an oath to defend the defenseless, even at the cost of his own life."

Ari Ara shrugged . . . such distinctions made little difference to the dead. It was cold consolation to orphans whether their father died under the sword of a warrior or a soldier.

"A Fanten shepherdess," Shulen repeated with a scowl. He stared at her for a long moment. An expectant hush fell over the assembly. Then he pinched a lock of her hair between his thumb and forefinger, easily blocking her incensed attempt to knock his hand away.

"Fanten do not have hair like yours," he pointed out.

"I am not Fanten," Ari Ara replied with a defiant tilt of her chin.

"Then what are you?"

"Ari Ara."

Not this. Not that.

Shulen tilted his head back and roared with laughter.

She blinked at him in surprise. *He can laugh?* she thought, stunned.

The old warrior held her at an arm's length and regarded her from head to toe. A strange expression crossed his face. His eyes narrowed with questions and a spark of light she could not interpret, as if hope and despair fought a battle behind his eyes. Finally, he said,

"You will be my apprentice."

"No."

The monks and orphans gasped at her defiance. Shulen raised an eyebrow.

"I'm only taking one."

"I've heard the Great Lady only has one dancing rat terrier - but that doesn't mean I want to be it," Ari Ara retorted, using a common Fanten saying.

Shulen hid a smile.

"Show some respect," Head Monk insisted, bustling over to them.

"Not until he does," Ari Ara muttered. She ducked under the cuff aimed at her head.

"I'm so sorry, Master Shulen - " the Head Monk started to say.

Shulen cut him off.

"Ari Ara of Monk's Hand, Fanten shepherdess of the High Mountains," he addressed her formally, "I will be standing here at daybreak tomorrow, ready to offer my skills and trainings," his lips twitched in wry humor, "which are not insignificant. If you should deign to grace me with your presence, I will rise to the challenge of teaching you."

Their gazes met and locked.

"I will only wait for you once," he added warningly.

Stone-grey and blue-grey eyes matched wills. Then she broke contact, twisted free, darted from the courtyard, and ran off into the black shepherd's cloak of night.

CHAPTER THREE

· · · · ·

"Master Shulen, please. There are far more qualified candidates. Many would be honored to be your apprentice. Young Brol, for example - "

Shulen waved the suggestion aside.

"The others will be very disappointed," Head Monk argued.

"Consider it warrior training," Shulen said unflinchingly. "They will have far greater disappointments in life."

Head Monk blustered on. Shulen sipped his tea and scanned the shelves of scrolls and books that lined the walls of the small office. The rest of the monastery slumbered while the two men discussed the redheaded girl who had so unexpectedly shown up that evening. Head Monk had spent the past hour attempting to dissuade the grey-haired warrior of the folly of his offer to the child.

"She's a half-wild creature who grew up tending sheep. She has no manners, no obedience, no discipline - "

Shulen interrupted the other man.

"A child does not live among the Fanten without cultivating a sort of discipline that puts ours to shame."

"Surely, you're not suggesting - "

"How many monks or warriors know how to eke out sustenance from the bare rocks and deep forests above us?" Shulen asked pointedly.

"She comes to eat our bread - "

Bread. Shulen snorted softly to himself. To a Fanten child, bread would seem a miracle. He carefully schooled his expression into a study of polite interest as the Head Monk listed the flaws in the girl. Shulen revealed no hint of his inner thoughts . . . even as his mind raced. The way that child moved! The girl had a natural ability unmatched by any trainee he had ever seen. She moved like the Fanten, quick, evasive, but with the determined stubbornness of a Marianan. A long-buried memory rose in his consciousness. He brushed it aside.

"Where did she come from?" he asked the Head Monk abruptly.

The portly man shook his jowls and folded his hands into his sleeves, frowning as he tried to remember.

"I don't know. It seems she was always here. I believe the Fanten found her. Years ago, the headwoman came to the monastery with her, saying something about how she wasn't of their blood and we had to take her. Everything was chaos in those days, as you'll remember - Queen Alinore dead, the heir missing, and war on the verge of breaking out. The Fanten headwoman stood in the courtyard - smack in the middle of everything - with this redheaded child in her arms, watching us with a sour expression. Then she just turned and left."

"They abhor war and violence," Shulen pointed out. "With all the preparations and deployment of warriors bustling around the monastery at that time, I'm not surprised she took the infant and disappeared. It would be unthinkable for any of the Fanten to leave a child in such a place."

26

"Well," the Head Monk huffed, "I forgot all about it. Years later, we started seeing her - hard to miss with that hair - and someone said she tended sheep. We caught her sneaking into the monastery one night, perhaps two years ago now. Ran away before we could speak with her."

"Do you think she'll come tomorrow?" Shulen asked.

The Head Monk blinked.

"I doubt it," he answered with a sigh.

The next morning, however, she was there in the darkness, waiting. Curled in a tight ball beneath the felted shepherdess cloak, she listened to the herald of the birds calling the sun to rise. She had slept lightly in a soft meadow, woken in the dark, and descended by sense and touch. Now, she crouched and waited, perched just outside the monastery gate on one of the carved stone warrior statues that flanked the entry.

Her ears prickled. The pulse of dawn dove into the bowl of night. The blackness shifted into midnight blue. Her eyes detected the first outlines of the boulders. She rose and stepped into the training sands of Monk's Hand Monastery. The mists hissed as they fell down the sides of the mountains and swirled around her. She felt the air move behind her and instinctively whirled.

"Very good," said Shulen. His voice was deep, but quiet. "You came."

"Yes," Ari Ara spoke, facing the stone-grey man.

"Why?" he asked.

"It sounded like a challenge," she answered. "I never back down from a challenge."

"Never?" he repeated with a slight smile of amusement. "What if you might lose?"

She shrugged. To lose was just a momentary setback.

"You can't lose if you never give up," she told the warrior defiantly.

"You can if you die," Shulen reminded her soberly.

Ari Ara sniffed.

"The Fanten say that's when the real adventure begins."

Shulen frowned at the saying, but did not argue further.

"Let's begin then," he told her.

"Begin what?" Ari Ara asked as twin jabs of eagerness and nerves struck her.

"You know about *Attar*, the Warrior's Way?"

She nodded. Everyone knew about that. Even the pig herder's sons in the village talked about it constantly. She had heard them on the days she descended from the High Mountains, and the obsessive chatter about *Attar* had driven her stiff with boredom last winter when she stayed in the village.

"And *Anar*?"

"The Weak's Way," she said dismissively.

Shulen corrected her sharply.

"Would you mock the elderly, the children, the new mothers, the frail? Might as well scorn your friend whose leg forces him to follow *Anar*'s way."

Ari Ara bit her bottom lip, glad that the pre-dawn greyness hid her blush.

"The Gentle Way is a better name," Shulen informed her. "Let there be no confusion on this point: the Gentle Way, *Anar*, is both the reason the Warrior's Way exists and the reminder of its failings. The Gentle Way avoids conflict. The Warrior's Way fights it. *Anar* and *Attar* are the great companions, the husband and wife of this world. She reminds him to stop fighting when it is time. Respect *Anar*, or else we will be lost to death and destruction and war."

Shulen paused, considering his next thought.

"*Anar* is also called the Way of Shadows, in contrast to *Attar's* Way of Blazing Fire. In this interpretation, the Fanten are masters of *Anar*."

"The Fanten?" the girl asked in surprise.

"Yes. They deal with conflict through secrecy and silence, hiding, disappearing, waiting and watching. But," he warned her, "don't be fooled. The Fanten are as powerful as the greatest warriors. Even as they yield and retreat, it is only to circle around to defeat their opponents from behind. Be very careful when dealing with them. Never underestimate their style of *Anar*."

"But," Ari Ara interrupted, "what if *Anar* doesn't take a stand when she should? What if she stands aside while harm is done to others? What if someone is going to get hurt?"

"With *Attar*, someone is always hurt," Shulen pointed out. "But there is a third way."

"There is?" Ari Ara retorted skeptically. "I've never heard of it."

"Hardly anyone has," Shulen sighed. "It has been secret since the descendants of the Third Brother disappeared. Do you know of the Three Brothers?"

Ari Ara nodded. The founders of the Desert People and the Marianans had been brothers. The third brother took no land or kingdom, but traveled between the others trying to keep peace. Once, long ago, his descendants tried to stop a war and were persecuted into hiding. No one knew much about them anymore.

"The Third Brother also had a way. It is called *Azar*, the Way Between."

Ari Ara frowned.

"In Fanten Tongue, *azar* means water," she said.

"Yes, or more precisely, it means *the way that water flows between obstacles without giving up*. Fanten language is very close to the Old Tongue, much closer than either the Desert Speech or the various dialects of Mariana."

Shulen paused. The first ray of light broke over the rim of the High Mountains and touched the head of Old Monk Mountain above the monastery.

"It is *Azar*, the Way Between, that I would like to share with you."

"Why?" she asked immediately.

Shulen's thin smile toyed with his lips. *Look at this one*, he thought, *she bristles at the smallest slight, yet does not recognize honors when they are handed to her.*

"There are only two living people who follow the Way Between," he explained to her. "One is an old warrior grey in the head and already alive long past his time. The other is sworn to throw himself in front of deathblows intended for the Great Ones."

"Emir Miresh?" she guessed.

"Yes. So, you see, *Azar* is on the brink of vanishing."

"But you could teach it to the whole monastery. Why me?"

"Because you demonstrated an inclination for it last night."

Ari Ara shifted from foot to foot.

"Why not teach me the Warrior's Way?"

"I would rather teach a fish to haul an oxcart," Shulen said with a tone of disgust.

Ari Ara bristled.

"You think I couldn't do it?"

"I know you couldn't," Shulen answered flatly. "No Fanten-raised child can be trained to hurt and kill."

Ari Ara scowled ferociously, but said nothing. It was true.

"*Ari Ara,*" Shulen drawled out her name, "neither this, nor that. One who can neither fight, nor flee. Even your name suggests that you should learn the Way Between. Will you study it?"

Shulen's voice rang out like a challenge. Ari Ara lifted her eyes to his.

"Yes."

"I will make you do trainings you will neither like nor understand," Shulen warned her.

"Fine."

"It will be harder than you can imagine."

"Try me."

"You will have to move into the monastery and obey its rules -"

"What?!" she yelped.

"I can't be chasing you up and down the mountains," Shulen explained, "I have thirty trainees and twice as many warrior monks to train."

"But - " Ari Ara stopped. She shrugged. She could do it; she could follow the rules even if she'd didn't like them.

"You will not train with the others. I will give you instructions for when I am occupied with other duties."

She nodded.

"Do you agree?"

"Yes," she answered resolutely.

"Then let us begin," Shulen replied.

The dawn mists swirled and thickened throughout the valley. In the chilly courtyard, the grey tendrils shifted, concealing and revealing the pillars and archways. The tiles of the roof gleamed with moisture. One morning soon, Ari Ara realized, they'd be patterned with white frost. She shivered.

Better to have to follow the monastery rules this winter than to be free and frozen in the High Mountains. Shulen spoke again.

"*Azar*, the Way Between, is about seeing what's not evident and moving in the space that opens between the obvious."

Shulen moved swiftly on his feet, brushing past her. She spun. He vanished into the mists. Ari Ara shifted her weight onto her toes, readying muscles to spring aside. She heard the crunch of his step to her right and felt his hand flip her hair as he flew past like the wind. He was gone again before she turned. She squinted, looking for Shulen. He tapped her on the shoulder. She whirled. The mists swallowed him.

She rotated in a slow circle, searching for him. Shulen darted out of nowhere and tapped her on the nose. She let loose a muffled cry of exasperation as he slid away again. *Those taps,* she thought ruefully, *could just as easily be blows.* The tiger was toying with her.

"Look for what's not there," his voice whispered in her ear.

The mists conspired against her and hid him once again. She narrowed her eyes. *How am I supposed to see what's not there?* she grumbled silently. Everything was cloaked in mists, shadows, dripping moisture, pooling damp spots. Shulen was nowhere to be seen. She frowned in concentration and shifted her vision, blurring the lines of what was present, letting it flow past her mind like a stream. Instead, she looked for what *wasn't* there . . . aha! She saw him a fraction of a second before his fingers tapped her under the chin. Ari Ara began to move. She slid through the mists, watching the spaces where he was not, calculating by elimination where he might be moving.

His hand sliced the air. She ducked under it. He moved away. She followed, stalking the tiger. She couldn't hide from him - not yet - but she could now keep track of him as he circled, using this odd way of seeing where he wasn't. She

dodged him. Then again. The third time, her fingers brushed his elbow as he passed. She heard him growl in surprise.

They moved like this for an hour until the mists stopped swirling up and down the mountain. She was out of breath and feeling slightly cross-eyed from concentration. He had not even broken a sweat.

"Very good, kitten," he said approvingly as the sun pierced the rising veils of mist.

"I'm not a kitten," she hissed.

Shulen laughed.

"Would you rather be a mouse?"

She scowled at him.

"I meant it with respect," he told her sincerely. "Keep practicing and you might one day grow into a tiger."

The morning bell rang out. The monks rose. Ari Ara stood, stunned by the very idea.

After breakfast, he had another challenge for her.

"Up," Shulen commanded, patting one of the narrow stone pillars that flanked the landing at the top of the long stairs to the monastery. The steps fell in a breathless sweep all the way down to the village. Behind the monastery, the steep slopes climbed the vertical heights. Hawks wheeled in slow circles above the peaks. Ari Ara turned to Shulen.

"On the ancestor stone?" Ari Ara questioned. "Isn't that bad luck?"

"No," Shulen replied with a short snort. "The monks just tell that to the orphans to keep them from breaking their necks."

Ari Ara folded her arms across her chest, as superstitious as the next.

"This is a traditional training. I've done it. Miresh did it."

"He did?"

"Yes, and he's not cursed, so get up there."

The pillar reached nearly to her chest. She eyed it, stepped back a few paces, took a running leap and hurtled up on top, catching her balance on one foot.

Shulen hid his impressed expression.

"Good. Now stay there."

Ari Ara tucked her free hanging foot up against her standing leg in a common shepherdess stance. She had spent hours watching the flock in the High Mountains, amusing herself by feats of stamina and balance. She grinned. She'd show him!

"How long?" she shot back with an arrogant tilt to her head.

"As long as you can," Shulen instructed her.

"I could stand here all day," she warned him.

Shulen raised an eyebrow.

"We shall see," he murmured.

She smirked. The craggy warrior pointed to the pillars beside her and tapped on the characters carved into the stones.

"Remember, we all stand on the shoulders of our ancestors," Shulen lectured. "If they stood upright and firm, we will have an easier time maintaining our balance in the world."

He pointed at a set of cracked and crumbling pillars.

"If they faltered, we will have a more difficult journey through our lives."

"Whose ancestor am I standing on?" she asked impertinently, tossing her curls out of her eyes.

"All ancestors are your ancestors, orphan. The landscape of your life was carved by their actions. Your life lays down a foundation for all those who will follow. Meditate on that while you practice balancing in the present, today."

Then he turned away and left.

The littlest orphans gathered around the pillar, curious.

"What are you doing?" they asked.

"Balancing," she answered.

"Why?"

"Why not?" she shrugged.

They watched for a while, then ran off to lessons and chores. Ari Ara observed the training in the courtyard, feeling for an odd moment that her life hadn't changed much at all. She was still standing on one foot, the other tucked up against her thigh, overlooking a scene in the distance. Only, instead of Fanten sheep, she watched warrior monks and trainees kicking each other.

At midday break, the session in the courtyard halted for a rest and a few of the trainees wandered over.

"You look ridiculous," snorted one.

What was his name again? she wondered. *Ah yes, Brol.* The one who did so well in the Trials. He stood tall, several years older than her, strong as the warrior monks, and skilled. Ari Ara disliked the sneer twisted on his face.

"Not half so ridiculous as you looked flailing around in those kicks," she snapped back. She mimicked him in the training session, exaggerating a particular move he had struggled to master. The others laughed. Brol glowered and stepped closer.

"Dodge this," he growled and swiped at her standing leg.

She hopped over his arm and landed neatly down on her other foot, securely balanced on the pillar. He moved to strike again, but Second Monk hollered at them to return to practice.

"This isn't over," Brol warned her.

No, she agreed, watching him go, *it has only just begun.*

At lunch, Teapot Monk spoke to Shulen.

35

"She's still standing there," he said, tilting his head toward the wiry child perched one-footed on top of the pillar.

Shulen glanced up.

"She'll give up and come down soon," he answered, unconcerned.

Teapot Monk gave him a worried look.

"It may take awhile," Teapot Monk mumbled, thinking of certain rumors he had heard from the villagers about the girl.

"Determined?"

"Very."

"Then we'll see just how determined, won't we?"

By midafternoon, she had switched legs several times, but showed no sign of coming down. She licked her lips and sucked her tongue to break the thirst, thinking of times during the High Mountain summers when the shallower springs dried up. She had learned to grit her teeth and suck stones and keep going until she found a fresh source.

By dinner, her knees were shaking. Her ankles burned along the tiny muscles required for staying balanced. The western sun pounded in her face and sweat rivulets trickled down her brow. When the sun vanished, the cold autumn breeze sent shivers down her spine.

The first stars emerged. Ari Ara wondered if she would have to stand here all night. She sighed, switched legs, and listened to the monks reciting evening chants. The rolling waves of Old Tongue washed over her. Her mind slipped into a half-trance, the kind the Fanten had spoken about for enduring pain or maintaining stamina over long distances. The stars spread into milky streams of time. The black waters of the ancestor river of the Fanten legends rose across the sky. Cloaked in the inky night, the Fanten spirits danced to the sound of the old monks' chanting. Step, step, sway; step, step, sway. Ari Ara rocked subtly in the motion of the silver-lined figures moving overhead. A fresh surge of energy tingled through her tired limbs. Then, without warning, the spirits vanished. The stars turned crisp and white above Old Monk Mountain. She sensed someone approaching in the dark.

"That's enough."

Shulen's outline appeared, backlit by the glowing lamps of the monastery. Ari Ara licked her lips and tried to speak. Nothing came out.

"Can you get down?" Shulen asked, drawing closer.

He decided not to find out and lifted the child from the pillar. Her knees buckled as he set her on the ground. He hauled her up by the elbow.

"Whoa!" he murmured softly. "You might have jumped down earlier."

"No," she croaked. "I said I could stand there all day."

"And so you can," Shulen acknowledged. "Now, let's get you some water, supper, and bed."

He would have to tread carefully with this one, he thought. Shulen smiled in the darkness. She had twice the grit of Emir Miresh at that age . . . though he'd never tell her that. If she managed to curb her temper and her tongue, she'd go far.

CHAPTER FOUR

. . . . .

Later that night, Ari Ara lay in her assigned cot in the trainees' hall achingly sore and wide awake. The press of people choked her, but she was determined to "obey all the rules of the monastery" as Shulen had instructed. She gritted her teeth and tried to count her breaths as the snores and lip smacks grated on her nerves. The ceiling seemed to compress the air straight out of her lungs. Finally, she rolled over, grabbed her thick shepherdess cloak and snuck out of the hall. She sat for a long time at the gate of the monastery, watching the stars revolve overhead. The cool air and the dark sky calmed her. At last, she curled under the cloak and slept.

Shulen's voice woke her at dawn.

"Why aren't you in the hall? You can't sleep out here."

She sat bolt upright and nearly knocked her head against one of the stone warriors that guarded the gateway of the monastery. Ari Ara rubbed the sleep out of her eyes. Shulen peered at her with a puzzled expression.

"Can't sleep in there either," she muttered, "too many dog-breath monk-boys."

Shulen cleared his throat in a bemused way.

"There's an empty hall closet in the senior monks' corridor," he started to say to tease her.

"I'll take it," she answered seriously.

"I was joking," he commented drily.

"I'm not."

He eyed her height.

"As long as you don't grow, you might just fit. The monks said I could use it," he explained, "though I doubt they intended me to store my apprentice in it."

He smiled at the humor and beckoned for her to follow.

The senior monks' corridor was a double line of tiny rooms that ran the length of the southeast side of the monastery, warmed by the extra sunlight and protected from the windy drafts that buffeted the west end. Beyond the first hallway, a second set of rooms was carved underground, dark and quiet. The wing of monks' quarters hung suspended in hushed silence. The air tingled with the accumulated energy of centuries of meditations. It reminded Ari Ara of the deep shadows of the Fanten Forest and she breathed a sigh of relief.

"You'll have to be quiet," Shulen warned her as they arrived.

The closet was a long set of shelves set into the corridor wall with a door that slid - like all the monastery doors - into the wall to conserve space. It was just long enough for a small child, deep enough for a bedroll, and high enough for her to use the lower shelf for a cot and the top shelf to hold her few belongings. Shulen pulled the middle boards out of the center and stacked them on the floor. Ari Ara spent a moment moving the sliding door back and forth almost reverently. It was the first room she'd ever had, if you didn't count meadows or mountains.

"If you don't like it," Shulen said, "you can move back into-"

"I like it," she said fiercely, spinning toward him with a fervent expression on her face. Then she whirled and ran off as the breakfast bell rang.

That afternoon, she discovered that she was expected to do chores just like the other orphans and trainees. Since she and Minli did not participate in the afternoon training sessions in *Attar,* they were often assigned duties together. She never imagined that life with the warrior monks involved so many mundane tasks. In the fading warmth of the autumn afternoons, they peeled root tubers for Nobstick, chopped herbs for Teapot Monk, swept the corridors, dusted scrolls, ground inks for the archivist, rinsed brushes for Scholar Monk, scrubbed robes, and a hundred other utterly boring tasks.

Meanwhile, the life breath of the monastery revolved around the warrior monks and trainees in the courtyard. The inhabitants of Monk's Hand Monastery lived, slept, breathed, and dreamed *Attar.* They argued strategy and techniques over lunch. They studied ancient scrolls on the great battles of the past. They honed their minds in singled-pointed meditations at dawn and dusk each day to build concentration for the chaos of the battlefield. They drilled every hour of the day.

No wonder the Fanten frowned on the warrior monks, Ari Ara thought as she and Minli spied on the practices from the sidelines. Every aspect of the monastery was devoted to fighting. She could just imagine the Fanten Grandmother's disgusted expression if she heard the long litany of prayers they chanted about winning victories over foes and slaughtering the enemy.

"Discipline, determination, dedication," Shulen barked at the trainees as they sweated through lunges and rolls. "The warrior must have all three. You will be exhausted, cold, hungry, near death, and still rise to the battle. The lives of others depend on you. Get up and keep going!"

His last comment was sent with a glare to a panting trainee who had stopped to catch his breath. The youth gulped and struggled to continue.

The trainees adored Shulen. He was tough. He was stern. He was the real thing. They counted his scars and whispered to each other about his battles. Ari Ara watched their eyes follow the Stone One's every move. She bit back her burst of laughter.

Shulen was interesting, she gave him that. But he was also crazy. They all were. There wasn't a single sane occupant of Monk's Hand Monastery - except possibly Teapot Monk who was more interested in baking a perfect loaf of bread than defeating an enemy. In Ari Ara's opinion, *Attar* involved far too many bruises and black eyes. But the trainees glowed as they obsessively reenacted, blow-by-blow, the battles of the past. They took a hard fall and leapt up for more. They pushed through pain and stoically endured grueling exercises. Ari Ara shuddered.

All of the trainees spied on Shulen's personal practices at dusk, but Ari Ara couldn't watch his drills without remembering that each sword slice was intended to slash living flesh, and every block or parry indicated another fighter's intention to kill him. The other trainees saw his prowess; she saw brutal, grim determination. *Attar* brought him no joy, she realized, even if he excelled at it. He left his personal practices in a dark mood, his eyes empty and hollow beneath his stony exterior.

The trainees gushed about his strength, speed, skill, and seemed oblivious to the severity and joylessness with which the warrior drilled. *But then*, Ari Ara thought to herself, *they'd never seen him any different*. The warriors-in-training had not seen the satisfaction she had glimpsed in his face during *Azar* practice. They probably didn't even suspect that the Stone One's eyes could gleam with contentment. *He may be the greatest warrior Mariana has ever seen*, Ari Ara reflected, *but that does not make him any happier.*

Shulen was right. She had too much of the Fanten in her to get caught up in the fascinations of warriors.

"Do they even know what war is?" she complained to Minli. "Do they have any idea what happens on the ground . . . when those practice kicks are real and swords are swinging not sticks? They act like this is all a game."

"It is a game to them," Shulen said, overhearing her comment. He had drawn closer as the youths sprinted back and forth across the courtyard in an exercise of agility and speed.

Ari Ara and Minli stared at him in surprise.

"It is taught to them as a series of games and playful competitions with honors and rewards for effort and success . . . because otherwise, no one would train for war. Either they are forced into battle for fear of their lives, or they must be raised on the milk of myths and the bread of war heroes, steeped in legends and fantasies."

Shulen sounded bitter.

"Why don't you tell them the truth?" she asked.

"Because then they would not train for war."

Minli swallowed nervously at the cold steel in Shulen's tone, but Ari Ara ploughed on fearlessly.

"Maybe we wouldn't have so many wars if we didn't train so hard for them."

Shulen's gaze fixed on the red-faced determination of the hardworking youths.

"And when the Desert People invade?" he challenged her. "What then? If we did nothing, we would be massacred."

43

Shulen stepped away before she could respond. Ari Ara glared at his back. *Maybe the Desert People wouldn't invade if the Marianans didn't attack them in the Border Mountains*, she thought grumpily. She couldn't wrap her mind around the one-sided thinking that pervaded Monk's Hand Monastery. Her logic stretched across borders and into the shared territories of the human heart.

Ari Ara imagined that, somewhere, a hawk-nosed desert warrior version of Shulen was also whistling through his fingers, halting the youths in their war practices, and telling them that constant dedication was the only thing that would save them and their families.

"Keep light on your feet," Shulen was telling them. "A warrior relies on speed and agility as well as strength and stamina. Concentration is vital - "

Shulen moved faster than a tiger springing for a kill. Brol toppled to the ground, gaping up at the older man.

"Pay attention," Shulen said simply, hauling Brol back up onto his feet. "A warrior's focus must be absolute. Do not let your mind wander or you'll be dead. Emir Miresh did not become Champion of Mariana by daydreaming in practice. Discipline, determination, dedication!" Shulen barked at them.

Ari Ara mimicked the phrase behind Shulen's back, putting her hands into fists on her hips exactly as he did. One of the trainees choked with laughter. Shulen did not turn around, but Ari Ara discovered he had eyes in the back of his head.

The next morning, he made her chant *discipline, determination, dedication* over and over as she climbed the boulder slide above the monastery at first light.

"Everything I teach in *Attar* applies doubly to an apprentice of *Azar*," he chided her when she ran back into the courtyard, breathless. "I expect you to work twice as hard as the others."

44

Ari Ara sourly replied, "I'd rather train in the afternoons than do endless chores."

Shulen frowned.

"You'll appreciate the extra practice at those skills later in life. The warriors-in-training are learning how to fight . . . but how many of them will know how to heal?"

The grey-haired taskmaster was either prophetic or he dropped a word in Teapot Monk's ear. That afternoon, the little round monk made Ari Ara and Minli grind up herbs and boil medicinal tinctures for the endless rows of jars of salves and ointments he kept on hand. By the end of the week, they had a working knowledge of how to remedy bruises, overworked ligaments, abrasions, cuts, twisted limbs, and the handful of colds and sniffles that the orphans passed around. Ari Ara was quietly impressed. Each morning, Teapot Monk rose to the challenge of creating miracles out of a busy schedule and too few hands. After that, though she still wriggled out of polishing the practice sticks or sweeping the training grounds, she attended to her chores for Teapot Monk with enough discipline, determination, and dedication to satisfy even Shulen.

Still, the obsession with *Attar* rankled her. From the toothless senior monks to the tiniest orphans, every inch of life was twisted to the purposes of training for war. *Give them a bolt of beautiful silk cloth*, she thought in disgust, *and the warrior monks would demonstrate how to strangle someone with it.* The older ones spoke of war, the trainees spoke of Trials, and the orphans played imaginary games about being the Lost Heir's Champion.

The orphans were raised on legends more than porridge, and indeed, among the children when the winter stores grew scant, many whispered stories to chase off the pinch of hunger. Who hadn't been scolded for daydreaming during chores about the missing child of Queen Alinore and the Desert King? The story was legendary; everyone had heard it a hundred times . . . just over the northwestern shoulder of the Old Monk, down the ravine on the other side, Shulen took his famous stand to give the Queen time to escape their pursuing attackers. Alinore struggled up the slope, heavy with child, labor pains starting. Shulen battled for her life - and was sliced into shreds and left for dead. He saved the Queen from the swords of the attackers, but not from exhaustion and fever. The Fanten found her body in one of their caves under the trees and discovered Shulen barely alive down the slope. The child was lost.

And, being lost, the rumors and speculation abounded. After all, many of the orphans were the right age to be the Lost Heir. Some of them remembered their parents; others did not. And, those deprived of memories of their mothers and fathers lulled themselves out of loneliness with dreams that *he or she* might be that lost child, and someday, officials from Mariana Capital would come to fetch them. Even if they were not the Lost Heir, they might still train hard and become the Champion of the Lost Heir, a warrior's honor second to none.

"Minli," Ari Ara mentioned in an awed tone as they swapped stories and scrubbed dishes in the kitchen. "You could be the Lost Heir."

"Don't be ridiculous."

"Don't be such an old monk," she retorted.

"Don't leave grime on the pots," he argued, pointing to the part she had missed, frowning as seriously as the senior monks.

"But you could be, you're the right age and you were left here at the monastery," Ari Ara insisted, staring off into space dreamily. "Any day now, the Great Lady Brinelle, Queen Alinore's cousin, could send her entourage to fetch you."

"Ari Ara," Minli said quelling, "you don't even know what an entourage is, and the Lost Heir is certainly not one-legged."

"How do you know?" she argued back, flicking the soapy water at him. "Maybe you lost it in the battle of Shulen's Stand."

"Nonsense," he retorted, splashing her, "the Lost Heir wasn't born yet when Queen Alinore fled up the slope."

"But maybe they tried to kidnap you and you lost it then."

"Why would the attackers cut off the Lost Heir's leg?"

"Maybe it was an accident."

"And why would they abandon the Lost Heir at the monastery?"

"Maybe the Fanten rescued you!" Ari Ara suggested enthusiastically.

"Maybe your story has too many *maybe*'s in it," Minli snorted.

"*Maybe*," interrupted Teapot Monk from behind them, "the Great Lady will come tomorrow for the both of you, one for Heir, one for Champion. But today, you're simply a pair of ordinary orphans with a very large stack of dishes to scrub."

And he flapped his hands at them to shoo them back to work.

Under the cover of the clank and rattle of the kitchen, Ari Ara whispered to Minli, "I think you are the Lost Heir; you even look a little like Queen Alinore."

"Really? Do you think so?"

"Yes, yes!"

Minli squinted at her suspiciously.

"How would you know? You never saw her."

She threw the dishcloth in his face. He upended his rinse water on her head. They burst into giggles that even Teapot Monk's scolding couldn't suppress.

Throughout the monastery, the Lost Heir was invoked as a charm against long days of working, lonely nights, the village children's teasing, and the hollow aches of an orphan's heart that no amount of chaos in a busy monastery could fill.

Each morning, Shulen woke her at daybreak, sliding open the door to the hall closet. She'd roll out and follow him quietly while the senior monks meditated and the orphans still slumbered in bed.

"What are we doing?" she had asked on the first day.

"Shhh, watch," he replied.

Shulen raised his hands, palms out, fingers touching, thumbs forming a triangle. He gestured for her to mimic the stance. She planted her feet slightly wider than her narrow hips and tilted her head back. She squinted across the grey bowl of the crater valley as they faced the jagged peaks of the High Mountains in the east.

"Feel it yet?" he murmured.

She frowned and shook her head.

"The day is coming. Get ready to catch it."

Suddenly, Ari Ara's skin prickled with the energy of the rising sun. The mists shifted. The greyness lightened. The clouds broke and a ray of light shot over the mountains, through her raised hands, and touched her chest squarely on her heart.

"Oh!" she gasped.

Shulen's smile curled.

"We never know what the new day might bring, but we can always be ready to greet it."

They stood silently as the sun poured through their fingers and flooded their limbs with warmth. The morning bell rang. Another day at the monastery began.

By midmorning, the training sands rang with shouts of *Attar!* The youth practiced parries and thrusts with wooden practice swords. As they drilled in long repetitions, Shulen found his mind tracing back over the years, calculating how many children he had trained into warriors, and how many of those had died in the battlefields.

A trainee glanced up, shuddered at the expression on Shulen's face, and hurriedly blocked his partner's swipe.

The Stone One stood in the middle of the training sands as the trainees lunged back and forth on all sides. His hands were clasped behind his back as he barked out reminders and instructions. He was only half-present; the lesson was grilled into his mind through practice. He could teach it in his sleep - and often did in nightmarish dreams where boys with wooden swords turned into men with steel blades and then into corpses clutching at nothing on blood-soaked battlefields. In some nightmares, he was a living corpse, a skeletal figure walking through a world of death. The frantic wives of slain farmers and goat herders rushed after him, pleading with him to spare their husbands and sons. Wherever their hands touched him burned with pain and fire.

Shulen snapped out orders to the trainees, setting them to another round.

Last night, *she* had come again. The images imprinted on his mind: long dark hair, midnight eyes, and the shadowed lines of her skin. *Run!* He had yelled, but she inevitably came closer as he wheeled and fought in the heat of the battle. *Get out of here, Rhianne!* He shouted at her, calling her name. Her eyes grew vacant with the horror of his wounds and the dead at his feet. He spun, sliced an attacker, and she screamed. He saw her fists clenched to her cheeks in fear of him - *him!* And behind her, he saw -

"Enough!" he hollered to the dream.

The trainees halted in surprise.

Shulen's face revealed nothing of his thoughts. These nightmares were not new. As he had so many times before, he covered his inadvertent cry by correcting the stance of the boy closest to him. Demonstrating the proper posture and footing, he made them all promise to pay closer attention. *So you can grow as old as me and live haunted by all that you've survived,* he thought bitterly.

He tried to keep his mind fixed on the exercise, but again, the woman flashed before his eyes. *You knew it would be hard,* he reminded himself sternly. Coming back to Monk's Hand after all these years to select and train guards, Shulen had known that the battle in the ravine over the ridge would haunt his dreams and distract his waking thoughts.

"Discipline, determination, dedication," he barked to the trainees and to himself.

He turned in a slow circle focusing on the young warriors. *Stay in the present,* he ordered himself.

Rhianne's laughter rang out.

He whirled.

On the landing beyond the courtyard, the redheaded girl was attempting to practice *Azar* while sweeping the stone steps. She had just tripped over the broom handle while trying to leap it, and laughed at her own foolishness. She climbed to her feet and tried again.

Shulen smiled, but it was a hard, aching twitch of lips.

Just that morning he had told her to practice *Azar* while doing her chores. It was an attempt to get her to do them in the first place . . . the girl constantly ducked out of her duties around the monastery. He had demonstrated his point on speed and spirals by using a broom to knock cobwebs down from the rafters in a whirl of motion.

"See?" he had said, handing over the broom. "Everything can be done with *Azar*, from the smallest task to moving the largest mountains. Indeed, the original practice of *Azar* was a dance, not a martial art. Using it solely for sparring is a waste of its potential."

Shulen pondered her thoughtfully, disconcerted by the familiar tone of that burst of laughter. He jerked from head to toe in a quick shudder to free him from the ghosts of his past. If he weren't careful, he'd see them walking in the living . . . and that was the gateway to insanity.

Ari Ara swept a pile of leaves to the side, launched over the broom handle, and landed neatly on the stone landing. A proud smile crossed her young face. Shulen nodded with inner determination as the young warriors-in-training fought and battled around him, preparing for war.

If he did nothing else good in this world, he decided, he would teach *Azar* to that girl.

CHAPTER FIVE

. . . . .

The one thing Ari Ara detested - more than scrubbing pots and far worse than the hardest exercises Shulen concocted - were lessons. Despite her protests, Shulen made her file into the Teaching Room with all the others. The low-roofed room was cramped with desks and chairs, and lined with shelves of books and scrolls. The air was musty from old records, punctuated by the sharp scent of wet ink. Ari Ara sat as close to the outside windows as possible and tried to avoid Scholar Monk's reprimands while daydreaming of the High Mountains. She would never, ever admit - to him or anyone else - that she could neither read nor write. Everyone would laugh at her. Even the littlest orphans could fill whole pages with brushstroke characters and copy basic scripts.

Day after day, she sat sullenly through her classes as Scholar Monk lectured about the chronology of historical wars, tactical maneuvers, and political stratagems of each dynastic epoch. While Minli and the others took avid notes in preparation for the end of the year exams, she willed her mind to absorb the dull information and prayed to whatever spirits were listening that no one would find out her secret. She tried, she really did, squinting at the squiggles for hours, hoping that they would snap into focus and reveal their hidden meanings. Nothing happened.

Bored brainless, Ari Ara clamped her mouth shut, folded her arms across her chest, and stared at the quivery mole on Scholar Monk's jowl. She attempted to follow the lecture, but sometimes she doubted Scholar Monk was even speaking Marianan amidst all the jargon and academic words. It slid in one ear and out the other by the time the noon bell rang.

"You haven't taken any notes," Minli pointed out at the end of the first week.

"I can remember everything," she retorted haughtily.

"You won't by the end of spring," he warned her. "Besides, Scholar Monk expects us to take notes."

So, Ari Ara started dabbling her brush in the ink and making lazy marks across her parchment.

"You'll get in trouble for doodling," Minli cautioned her.

She told him that it was Fanten script and slid it out of view, hoping he didn't know that the Fanten maintained an oral tradition by choice, rejecting the written forms prized by the Marianans.

When Scholar Monk swept down the aisle looking down the arch of his beak nose and holding out his hand for the essay they were supposed to write on the major battles of the Fifty Year War, she answered boldly,

"I didn't do it."

He demanded an explanation.

"It was a matter of life and death," she answered.

"Oh?" he retorted, unconvinced.

"Yes," Ari Ara replied, lifting her pointed chin. "I thought I'd die of boredom if I did it."

The students burst into laughter. Scholar Monk was not amused.

Ari Ara was assigned kitchen duties for a week.

She was scrubbing away at her hundredth pot when an orphan ran in from the courtyard, ducked down at her feet and crawled into the huge, dripping kettle she had just set down.

"Get out of there! I just washed that!"

"Shhh," the orphan begged, "we're playing Search for the Lost Heir. Don't give me away."

Ari Ara rolled her eyes and straightened up. The younger orphans adored the game, which involved hiding in obscure corners, running away from the team of desert demons that came to take them captive, being rescued by the opposing team of Marianan warriors, and trying to be the last "Lost Heir" hidden when the Searcher finally rounded everyone else up.

She sniffed disdainfully. They had never asked her to play. Ari Ara tried to act as if she thought the game was nonsense, but there were times when she wished that she could run shrieking and laughing around the monastery grounds with the rest. Minli held steadfast in his friendship, but other trainees and orphans eyed her as warily as they would a wild beast that had snuck in from the mountains. She suspected someone was spreading rumors about her - she could hear the trainees whispering behind her back. She caught snatches of phrases such as "shouldn't be here" or "she's not a real trainee".

The two girls who had passed Trials ignored her, joining the tight cohort group of older girls who were also training. They all sat together at meals and the one time Ari Ara had tried to join them, they told her bluntly to go away.

"We're talking about *Attar*," the oldest stated condescendingly. "You wouldn't understand. Go sit with the cripple."

Furious at her rudeness toward Minli, Ari Ara retorted, "Fine, he's worth ten of you, anyway."

And she turned her back on them as solidly as they snubbed her. The little orphans treated her with wary respect, but were shy of inviting her to their games. She was older than most of them, and Shulen's apprentice besides. They mostly ignored her and played among themselves.

Ari Ara rinsed the next giant pot and set it down beside the one the girl was hidden within. Another orphan barreled through the kitchen door and began searching through the cluttered shelves and closets. Ari Ara ducked down.

"Who's the Searcher?" she murmured to the hidden girl.

"Minli," the child whispered back.

"Keep quiet, then. There's a desert demon who's about to catch you."

Ari Ara stood up and put the lid on the huge pot. She sat down on top and started scrubbing dejectedly.

The other orphan approached.

"Seen anybody hiding in here?" he asked.

"Me?" she grumbled, evading the question Fanten-style. "I've been stuck in here scrubbing pots. Teapot Monk said he wanted to see his face shine."

The orphan made a sympathetic noise.

"If you're nearly done," he offered hesitantly, "you could join in. We've only just started. I'll give you a twenty-second count before I tell the others you're in."

Ari Ara glanced around. The kitchen monks were nowhere in sight.

"Alright," she agreed.

The boy darted out of the kitchen. She peeked into the pot. The little orphan grinned back.

"I'm going to hide," she told the girl. "Good luck."

56

She ran out the side door and into the corridor. Looking left and right, she ruled out the Main Hall, the copy room, and the archives . . . there had to be half a dozen orphans hiding in each by now. Ari Ara spotted a door on the far side of the kitchen. Head Monk's office! Perfect. No one entered there without express permission.

She tiptoed closer and put her ear to the door. Nothing. She slid it open a crack and peeked inside. No one. Cheering her good luck, she slipped into the office and cast around for a hiding place. Aha! In the corner, a large cupboard for scrolls and ceremonial robes stood unlocked. She opened the doors and crouched down at the bottom, covering herself with the scarlet of the fabric.

A few seconds later, she heard the door open. She cursed silently. They had found her so fast! Ari Ara pressed an eye to the slit between the wooden cupboard doors.

"They act like it's a game," Shulen's voice muttered in an irritated tone.

"They're children," Head Monk replied soothingly.

"No one will find it amusing if the Lost Heir isn't found soon," Shulen grumbled as Head Monk calmly poured him a cup of tea. The warrior's face was lined and scowling.

"So, the rumors are true?" Head Monk queried.

"Depends on what you've heard," Shulen answered with a sigh. "Rumors are churning thicker than mud along the Mari River. Our nobles claim the Desert King is hiding the heir. The desert factions are accusing us of the same. Both militaries are threatening to invade."

"Reminds me of the old days," Head Monk said with a bitter sigh. "Each side blaming the other, neither certain of the truth."

Shulen sipped his tea moodily and did not answer.

"Will there be war, do you think? Or is it just the usual blustering?" Head Monk asked after a pause.

Shulen drummed his fingers on the desk.

"I hope not, but the nobles are shouting about the need for a War of Reclamation . . . as if the War of Retribution after Alinore's death wasn't horrific enough."

"Let's pray they come to their senses," Head Monk moaned softly.

Shulen snorted.

"Let's pray we find the Lost Heir before the nobles convince the Great Lady to invade the desert again."

Ari Ara bit her bottom lip, worried. Great Lady Brinelle was not known for her diplomacy. She was Queen Alinore's cousin, daughter of Elsinore's sister, and ruled the nation in trust for the missing child . . . or for her son, Korin, who stood next in line for the throne. There were some who claimed Great Lady Brinelle made only half-hearted efforts to find Queen Alinore's child, but that was tavern talk that no one dared repeat too loud.

"Are there any leads at all?" Head Monk asked. "We've combed these mountains for answers, as you know. Not a sign or hint of the child."

"Have you asked the Fanten?" Shulen asked.

Head Monk made a disparaging noise.

"Oh, you know them . . . never a straight answer. They clam up tight as cider barrels and vanish into the forest."

"The Fanten Grandmother knows more than she says," Shulen told him.

"You could ask her," Head Monk suggested without much hope.

"She won't speak to me. She won't even come near me after-" Shulen broke off with a hard expression on his face. "I could search the forest for a hundred years and never glimpse her if she does not wish to be seen."

Ari Ara grinned. That was certainly true! She wondered how well Shulen knew the Fanten Grandmother. It sounded like they had a long history . . . and not all of it pleasant. She waited, but Shulen did not elaborate. Ari Ara sat back in the cupboard, thinking. Why wouldn't Fanten Grandmother speak to Shulen? The Fanten had been the ones to find him and heal him after the battle in the ravine. She made a small shrugging gesture. The Fanten held onto secrets as tightly as nobles hoarded jewels.

When Head Monk and Shulen finally finished their tea and left, her legs ached with cramps and tingled from falling asleep. She stumbled out of the cupboard and went looking for Minli, completely forgetting that he was the Searcher in the game. She was caught and had to wait impatiently through three rounds of rescues by mock warriors before the dinner bell rang. As the desert demons declared victory, having captured more "heirs" than remained in hiding, Ari Ara grimly remembered Shulen's caution: it would not be amusing if the two nations went to war over the Lost Heir. Not at all.

CHAPTER SIX

. . . . .

Ari Ara stood motionless between the boulders that lay jumbled to the south of the monastery. Her toes splayed in a small patch of sun-warmed sand. The giant stones of the old boulder slide were riddled with pockets of space. The warrior monks used them for small practice grounds; the trainees sparred here in their spare time.

Ari Ara was not sparring. In fact, she appeared to be doing absolutely nothing. Her eyes were shut and, except for the thin line of concentration running through her forehead, she seemed to be dozing off on her feet.

She was listening to the wind.

After lessons this morning, Shulen had tapped her on the shoulder.

"Go learn *Azar* from the wind," he told her.

She had rolled her eyes at his vague instructions, certain that he was just getting her out from underfoot. She was, however, obstinately determined to prove to him that one could do it.

The task was not so simple as it sounded. The air hung still and breathless. Barely moving, it tiptoed through the valley with only the faintest hint of motion. The light breeze was worse than Shulen on the first morning of her training, darting and disappearing, tickling her skin then vanishing. She closed her eyes and tried to sense the subtle currents that ran the length of the mountains. She knew they hung like invisible ribbons from peak to valley floor. Her limbs tingled with concentration.

There! The breeze touched her nose and for the first time all afternoon, she caught more than just the impression of its breath. It came from the northeast and the village, carrying the scent of bread and sheep and fields.

A cooler slip of air tickled the back of her ear. This one tumbled from up high, as if the Old Monk's cold breath fell from the peak. In her mind's eye, she pictured the hawks that often wheeled in circles near the top. They followed the unseen, ever-changing roads of wind that spun through the sky. Mimicking them, she spread her arms and splayed her fingers like the tips of the hawks' wings.

A snort of derisive laughter made her jump.

Brol leaned against the nearest boulder, arms crossed over his chest, scorn in his eyes. Ari Ara scowled back with equal animosity, disliking every strand of dark hair on his head and every inch of his pale skin. She had felt his scowl stabbing her in the back ever since Shulen chose her as his apprentice. Had she ever caught a clear glimpse of his resentment, she might have seen the jealousy burning in him as she usurped a position he felt rightfully belonged to him. He had trained, after all. He had studied. He had received the highest score at the Trials. But then she had waltzed down from the mountains, uninvited, with her impudent tongue and arrogant ways and stolen the apprenticeship. He shoved the vulnerable heat of his bitterness out of sight, though he couldn't quite conceal his dislike of the mouthy, self-righteous shepherdess.

"Learning to fly, Fanten brat?" he mocked, his mouth twisting into a sneer. "Flap your chicken wings hard enough and you might make it back to the desert where you belong."

"What are you talking about, Brol?" Ari Ara retorted, planting her fists indignantly on her hips. "I've lived here longer than you have, lowlander."

Brol ignored the jab. Most of the orphans were from the lowlands of Mari Valley or the Border Mountains closer to the desert. They were sent to Monk's Hand by charitable societies to ease the overcrowding in the central orphanages.

"Raised here, yes," Brol answered, smirking, "but with hair like a desert demon, you couldn't have been born here."

"The Fanten had me at infancy," she informed him haughtily, though she could not deny that many of the Desert People shared her bright copper hair. Even her skin ran a shade dark for Marianan blood. She didn't point that out, however. Fanten had darker skin than Marianans, too.

"Too bad you didn't drown in all the rain. Desert demons don't swim, you know," he told her.

"Must have some Marianan blood then," Ari Ara shot back, "because you could sooner drown a fish."

"Perhaps we should try," Brol said nastily. "We could hold you and a fish underwater to see who lives the longest."

Ari Ara glared back.

"Go shove your head in the well," she muttered.

"Tsk. Tsk. A little drowning might dampen that nasty desert temper of yours."

"Did it ever occur to you, Brol," she snapped, "that the Lost Heir might have a nasty desert temper, too?"

"Oh! Look who thinks she's the Lost Heir!" Brol howled with laughter.

"I didn't say that," Ari Ara retorted. "I'm pointing out that you're training to defend a half-Desert heir."

Brol's face snapped shut over his thoughts. His eyes narrowed. His laughter turned cold.

"That's what you think, brat."

He lunged to strike her, but she leapt to the side.

"Your mother was a desert dog," he snarled at her.

"How dare you!" she shouted, hurtling out of the way of the kick that accompanied the insult.

"How else did you get that hair?" he mocked her.

"You have no idea who my mother was!" she growled through gritted teeth, dodging him again.

"Neither do you," he replied, circling for another strike.

Her temper snapped. She whirled to hit him, but he was bigger, stronger, and faster. His leg shot out and caught her fury-blind lunge in the ribs.

She dropped to the sand, gasping. Brol's voice growled in her ear.

"Fly away, demon, get out of here."

Then he turned on his heel and was gone.

When she winced back into the monastery, Shulen raised an eyebrow, but she simply muttered that she had wrenched something while practicing.

She redoubled her efforts to learn *Azar,* pushing herself harder than before. Brol smirked as he watched her as if he saw through her seeming dedication to her practice . . . but he also increased his own efforts. He surpassed the other trainees in their lessons, and started winning more sparring matches in the evenings with the younger warrior monks.

Brol may have added intensity to her efforts, but it was her sheer fascination with *Azar* that rolled her out of bed each morning, eager for the next lesson. Shulen had a dancer's grace to his teachings that never emerged in the warrior trainings of *Attar*. It was with Ari Ara at dawn that a whole other side of the man slid out from under his stony exterior. Shulen's lessons unfolded in an exquisite exploration of beauty and motion. He taught her the seven ways to roll, and more importantly, the principles of falling and landing. Muscles are cushions, he told her, and by pouring your weight through them, you can soften your landing and rebound swiftly. Bicep, thigh, and outer calf each offered a landing and launch pad.

"Inside the structure of the body is a field of limitless possibility," he told her, "and it is the solid parameters of tendon and marrow, breath and blood, that allow the infinite to unfold."

He made her practice balancing on her feet, hands, shoulders, and more. Then, he made her pour her weight from one balancing point to another, faster and faster in a wild improvisation of falling and stillness. He taught her to spring in the ten directions, pushing off any point of contact. Each move opened the door for more . . . and she was as inquisitive as she was observant. She folded and curved around space and motion in an easy, loose agility. She let go of concepts of front and back, top and bottom, and moved only between. Head, feet, side, arms, legs: any piece of her could thread the rest of her body through the open eye of the needle of *Azar*.

Shulen found himself almost bored with the trainings of the young warriors. He drilled them adequately, but perfunctorily. Disturbed, he joined the older warrior monks in their evening practice sessions, but that only emphasized his growing dissatisfaction with the vast gulf of differences between *Azar* and *Attar*. The warrior monks were powerful, strong, fast, forceful, and skilled. They kept their heads up, feet down, and swords moving. He ran circles around them, hardly breaking a sweat. Shulen left the evening session feeling flat and disappointed.

With the girl, the world opened like sunlight after a hard rain. Possibilities glistened and shimmered in all directions. Ari Ara learned swiftly, ferociously, as if she had been starving for this her whole life. As for the Stone One, he remained as inscrutable as ever, but beneath his surface, a thousand pinpoints of change prickled under his skin. Shulen still toyed with her like a tiger teasing a kitten, but his trainings increased in speed and intensity, matching her pace. Ari Ara suspected that he had reserves of strength and stamina that he never revealed - not with her and not even when training the monastery's best warrior monks in the finer points of *Attar*.

Her lessons in the Teaching Room, however, remained an infuriating puzzle of squiggles on parchment. She was constantly in trouble with Scholar Monk. By the end of the first month, she was on the verge of skipping out on lessons to slip off into the High Mountains to avoid the agony of the classes.

"Ari Ara, come to the front," Scholar Monk ordered one day, equally frustrated with her.

The girl sighed and slid off her seat, walking the length of the classroom up to the front. Scholar Monk waited, trying to recall if she had completed a single assignment since she had begun taking lessons. He scowled at the fiercely obstinate expression on the redheaded child's face. He would have to speak to Shulen about her. He was reaching the limits of his patience. Scholar Monk pointed to the thick manuscript lying on his desk.

"Read the section on the feud between the Brothers that led to Marin and Shirar splitting the world," he ordered.

The other students stared at her. She could sense Brol's smirk in the back row. She swallowed and her blue-grey eyes flicked rapidly around the crowded room, searching for an escape route. Minli bit his bottom lip, nervous for her sake. Ari Ara shifted her feet and stared blankly at the markings on the page, her mind furiously racing. She felt the red flush of shame creeping up the back of her neck. Then, decisively, she shook her hair out of her face and wrinkled her nose.

"Everyone knows this story already," she complained boldly. "Why don't we ever learn about anything interesting like the Lost Heir?"

She had meant it only as a distraction, a wild attempt to get so far into trouble with her flippant comments that Scholar Monk wouldn't find out she couldn't read the text in front of her, but the older man blinked in surprise.

"But this has everything to do with the Lost Heir," he replied.

"How?" Ari Ara challenged immediately, stalling for time.

"It lays the foundation for the fissures of the nations and the Prophecy of the Lost Heir," Scholar Monk informed her sternly.

"The what?"

The room sat up straighter. Evidently, Ari Ara noted, she was not the only one for whom this was news.

"That's advanced study," Scholar Monk said in a quelling tone.

"There's a prophecy?" she pushed.

"Only the highest scholars and the Great Ones are allowed to know it. You will have to study a great deal harder if you wish to hear it someday."

With an exasperated look, he shooed her back to her seat. She darted away, relieved to be off the hook. Scholar Monk wiped his glasses, cleared his throat, and began to read the record. Ari Ara's thoughts raced excitedly. She'd give her shepherdess cloak to know what was in the Prophecy of the Lost Heir! If Scholar Monk wouldn't tell them, then it had to be absolutely fascinating.

"What do you think it says?" she asked Minli as soon as the noon bell released them from class. They had been assigned to beat the carpets from the senior monks' quarters. A heap had been brought out earlier in the day and stacked by the north side of the monastery. The afternoon was cool, but sunny, and as they pounded and shook the dust from the carpets, the heaviness of the thick wool rugs soon had them flushed despite the chill in the breeze.

"Something horrible," Minli answered, sneezing on the dust. "Otherwise, why would they keep it a secret?"

"Seems crazy to have a prophecy they won't tell anyone," Ari Ara concurred. "I wish we could at least see it."

"Why? Think you'll find something the best scholars have missed?" Minli teased.

She whacked the carpet paddle on the rug and sent a puff of dust into his face.

"You never know," she muttered. "It might say, *the Lost Heir has only one good leg,* but the monks just want to keep your tidy handwriting around here forever!"

Minli grinned at her nonsense and shook the edge of the carpet harder. Ari Ara stopped to cough and rub the grit out of her eyes.

"Bet they have a copy," Minli said absently.

"Who?" she asked. "The monks?"

"Yeah, here in the archives. Monk's Hand Monastery is the most esteemed records hall outside of the library in Mariana Capital, you know," the boy informed her proudly. His copies sat alongside those of the finest scribes in the dark and cool chambers where the records were kept.

Ari Ara raised her eyebrows.

"Where would it be?" she asked, shaking the end of the carpet with a heave.

"In the innermost records room where the most important scrolls are kept." Minli threw her a suspicious look. "You'd get into a lot of trouble for breaking in there."

Ari Ara shrugged. What was more trouble on top of the heap she was always in?

"Just think," she argued, "if the Lost Heir was found, it might stop the war."

"What war?" Minli asked.

She told him what she had overheard in Head Monk's office the day she hid in the cupboard.

"Do you really think they'll go to war?"

Ari Ara shrugged.

"Shulen thinks so . . . he says the nobles are already calling for a War of Reclamation to take back the missing child."

Minli bit his lip pensively.

"Then we'll have to find the Lost Heir first. I'll get the key to the records room."

"You'll what?!" she yelped, dropping the rug. "How?"

"Second Monk has one. I'll just tell him that Scholar Monk wants me to work on preserving some of the old scrolls. I've been in there before, once or twice. They made me copy over a bunch of the mildewing records this year."

"But there must be thousands of scrolls," she groaned. "We'll never find it."

Minli stared at her as if she'd grown up under a rock.

"They're labeled," he informed her. "Ordered by date, original scribe, subject, and location where they were recorded."

Minli rolled up his carpet. Ari Ara contritely grabbed the bulk of its awkward weight and helped stack it in the pile of clean rugs.

They plotted for three days, contriving to be assigned chores together during afternoon trainings and waiting for Minli to get the key out of Second Monk's hands. One afternoon while the senior monks were absorbed in another endless meditation, Minli hobbled around the corner to where Ari Ara was polishing the metal plates of shields and mouthed *now*, holding up the key. They tiptoed past the open doors of the Teaching Room where the younger orphans were practicing brushstrokes. Cautiously, they slid past Shulen and the trainees in the courtyard. Ari Ara felt the grey man's eyes boring into her back suspiciously. Quietly, they crept down the corridor behind the Main Hall, into the archives, and through the stacks. Ari Ara had never been this deep into the catacombs that burrowed into the belly of Old Monk Mountain. The air was perpetually cool and dry, eerily still and muffled.

Minli was about to put the key into the door of the innermost records room when the old archivist turned around the corner.

"What are you two doing?" he frowned.

"Uh," Ari Ara stammered.

"Dusting," Minli answered, using his robe to wipe the shelf nearest to him. "We were assigned to wipe all the shelves."

"It was a punishment," Ari Ara added. She quickly copied Minli's gesture.

"Now that, I can believe," the archivist sniffed. "What did you do this time?"

Ari Ara's mind stalled again.

"She whacked Scholar Monk with the flyswatter and told him that his mole looked like a fly," Minli explained with an innocent look.

The archivist's lips twitched.

"That was very naughty," he chided Ari Ara. She tried to look repentant. Then he frowned at Minli. "Why are you here?"

"He's supposed to keep an eye on me," Ari Ara explained hastily.

The archivist nodded. That, too, was believable, given the girl's reputation.

"Use a rag, not your robe," he ordered them. Then he picked out the scrolls he had been searching for and left.

They sighed in relief.

Ari Ara kept watch while Minli unlocked the door of the inner chamber. It creaked loudly as it slid back. They winced, but no one came running. The pair slipped inside the room.

Ari Ara held a lamp aloft while Minli searched the rows of neatly labeled scrolls and manuscripts. He strained his neck as he looked higher and higher.

"It's up there, I think," he said finally. "It should be the third roll from the right, top shelf."

Ari Ara handed him the lamp. Her heart pounded so loudly in her ears that she half-suspected the archivist would hear it drumming. She scaled the wall of scrolls, placing her bare toes carefully on the carved shelves to avoid crushing the delicate manuscripts.

"This one?" she hissed, pointing.

Minli nodded.

She slid it out and passed it down to him. She descended quickly, careful not to jump and make noise. Minli unrolled it reverently as she held the lamp again.

"Careful," he warned, "don't spill the oil on the scroll."

The script was in Old Tongue, not Marianan.

"This one is a copy of the original in the Capital," Minli said, reading a recent note in the upper corner, "but it's still very old."

He paused in surprise.

"It's Fanten . . . I mean, the prophetess was Fanten."

Ari Ara rolled her eyes. Surprise. Surprise.

"What does it say?" she whispered.

Minli didn't answer immediately. His eyes grew wider.

"Come on, read it," she urged, rubbing her eyes as if she had trouble seeing in the dim light.

"One will come, a child born of two lineages, mother dead, father distant. Lost at birth, appearing half grown, this child shall inherit two thrones, one in the desert, the other on the water. Uniter, Divider, Liberator, Destroyer; floods follow in this one's footsteps; famine stalks the heels of the heir. Upheaval and conflict surround this child, a war breaker, change maker. By the Mark of Peace, the lost one is found. Then the once broken becomes whole; the once wounded healed, and the once forgotten remembered again."

Ari Ara blinked.

"Why do they bother keeping this a secret?" she wondered.

"Because," said a voice behind them, "there are some who would rather control a piece of a broken world than share the whole world with everyone."

Ari Ara screeched and nearly dropped the lamp. They whirled. Shulen stood in the doorway with a stern expression. They gaped at him, too startled to speak.

"Your light showed in the corridor," he pointed out.

Shulen held out his hand for the scroll. Minli guiltily handed it over. Shulen's stony eyes took on a terrible darkness as he scanned the lines with a somber familiarity. He let out a long sigh.

Ari Ara and Minli squirmed.

"We were just, uh, dusting," Minli mumbled half-heartedly.

"And happened to find this particular scroll?" Shulen probed with a glint of amusement. "I think not."

"How much trouble are we in?" Ari Ara dared to ask.

"If I were a monk, quite a lot. It's a punishable offense to view this prophecy without permission or even to speak of its contents."

The children exchanged worried looks.

"Punishable by what?" Ari Ara wanted to know.

"Death."

Shulen glared at them sternly.

"But, you are fortunate today, orphans." Shulen rolled up the scroll carefully and returned it to the top shelf. "I've never thought that prophecy should be kept secret. Indeed, for most of history, it wasn't. This particular prophecy was simply another mildewing, irrelevant, obscure vision forgotten in the bowels of the archives. But then Queen Alinore fell in love with Tahkan Shirar, the Desert King, and a scholar remembered the prophecy. When the Queen died and a child of two lineages went missing, Great Lady Brinelle ordered it to be kept secret to prevent every ambitious noble in the country from placing the Mark of Peace on his or her child. There are only a few people who know about the prophecy, and an even smaller handful who have read its contents."

They looked at him in surprise.

"My advice, young ones," he cautioned them, "is that you forget what you have seen and go back to whatever chores you were assigned."

He turned them by the shoulders and prodded them out the door. Minli handed over the key sheepishly and Shulen locked it. He shooed them out of the archives. They scurried off as fast as Minli's leg allowed.

However, they would sooner stop breathing than not talk about the prophecy. A few minutes later, they whispered furiously back and forth as they polished the shields Ari Ara had abandoned earlier.

"What do you think it meant, *by the Mark of Peace, the lost one is found?*" Ari Ara asked.

"It means that the heir's got an identifying mark, something that proves he or she is the Lost Heir," Minli answered.

"But, what is the Mark of Peace?"

"It sounds vaguely familiar," Minli mused, his eyes glazing over in thought. "I might have read about it."

"Minli," Ari Ara groaned, "you've read the whole archive hall twice over."

"I could ask Scholar Monk - "

"Are you crazy?!" Ari Ara hissed. "Shulen said it was death to read it. We can't tell anyone!"

"Then face it," Minli sighed. "We're as unlikely to *find* the Lost Heir as we are to *be* the Lost Heir."

"Less chatter, more sorting," Nobstick scolded them as he walked past.

They waited until he was out of earshot.

"What was that part about *lost at birth, appearing half-found?*"

"Grown," Minli corrected. "Appearing half grown."

"Like a dwarf?"

"No, dense head," Minli answered, rolling his eyes. "It meant that the Lost Heir will reappear half grown up."

"You mean, like an adolescent?"

74

"Maybe younger," Minli amended. "Grown could be in reference to height or age or full maturity."

"Full maturity? How old is that?" Ari Ara asked.

"Well, the royal line comes of age in Mariana at twenty-four, but in the Desert, I think they have an adulthood ceremony at eighteen."

"So, there's a range," Ari Ara pointed out. "The Heir could be . . ."

"Between twelve and nine," Minli said. "Queen Alinore died eleven years ago. If the Lost Heir's still alive, the time for his or her reappearance is now. Maybe that's why Shulen's specifically training warriors for the Guard."

Or maybe he's preparing warriors for a War of Reclamation in the desert, Ari Ara thought, staring at the training sands where the youths were sparring ferociously. Along the sides, warrior monks cheered them on with shouts and battle cries. Ari Ara soberly pictured the boys fighting Desert People instead of each other.

"Minli," she said quietly. "We've got to find that heir."

CHAPTER SEVEN

. . . . .

Soon, the crack of cold stung the air each night. Frost fell from the heights of the mountains and gripped the bowl of Monk's Hand. The water barrels bore thin layers of ice in the mornings. One late afternoon, Ari Ara emerged from her chores in the kitchen to see the senior monks huddled in a cluster of deep grey robes. The heat of their breath rose on the frigid air. They broke apart and murmured to the older trainees, sending them scurrying across the courtyard.

"Did you hear?" Minli commented enthusiastically when she brought in her dinner bowl and sat next to him on a long bench in the dining hall. "The Fanten are beating their drums. The gate of autumn closes and the door of winter opens."

Ari Ara ran to the doorway and listened. A low pounding rumbled out of the forest. She gulped down her soup as the trainees brought armloads of deadwood into the middle of the courtyard, preparing a bonfire for sunset. In the forest, the Fanten would dance the autumn dances from dusk until dawn, she knew, feeding their ceremonial fire with fallen branches from the Great Trees. Down below, the villagers would hear the Fanten drums and light a fire in the village center. Up here at the monastery, the senior monks would chant the names of the ancient lineages. In the darkness of night, the ancestor ghosts would gather.

The Horns of Monk's Hand sounded as the sun touched the western shoulder of Old Monk Mountain. The Fanten drums halted for a breath, acknowledging the Horns through silence. Ari Ara shivered at the lingering reverberations of the low moaning sounds. In previous years, she had heard them mostly from a distance. Even in the Fanten Forest, the tremors could be felt underfoot. Here, the sonorous cries deafened her ears.

"Stay close tonight," Shulen warned her. "When the ancestors start walking in the mountains, strange things happen."

"That's just a child's tale," she scoffed.

He raised his grey eyebrows at her.

"Not all my scars come from mortal hands," he said in such a serious tone that Minli squeaked in fear.

"He's just trying to scare us," Ari Ara whispered to Minli as Shulen turned away. But, she inched closer to her friend and watched the growing darkness nervously.

Strange things did happen this time of year, she admitted quietly to herself. Even the Fanten kept close to their ceremonial fires on this night. She decided not to test the ancestors.

The senior monks gathered under the tiled overhangs of the three-sided courtyard, settling cross-legged. The oldest ones looked on the brink of departing for the spirit world, Ari Ara thought. The trainees and orphans gathered behind the senior monks on the benches that lined the walls. Bundled in robes and cloaks against the cold night, their huddled figures appeared eerily misshapen.

Suddenly, on one breath, the senior monks began to chant in low growling tones that rolled and groaned as if the stones of the river had learned to speak. They started with the names of the Three Brothers: Marin, Shirar, and Alaren, then the sons and daughters of the first two brothers, and the royal lineages they founded. *What about the Third Brother?* Ari Ara wondered. *Why don't they recite his children?* The litany would continue until dawn, Minli informed her, the younger monks taking over for the older monks until the orphans spoke the name of Alinore to the rising sun. The Desert King and the Lost Heir would not be named . . . not until they passed into the spirit realms. *What will they do a thousand years from now,* Ari Ara wondered, *when the list is too long for a single night? Chant faster?*

Head Monk stepped forward holding a flaming torch aloft. The leaping light and pulse of voices swirled around him. His red ceremonial robes seemed to be woven into fire, bloodlines, and the ancestor spirits. He spoke in Old Tongue and then set the torch to the base of the bonfire. It erupted. Flames leapt above the roofline of the monastery. Ari Ara gasped. She stared wide-eyed at the towering fire, secretly relieved that the stone buildings stood no chance of catching aflame. The ferocity of the fire sent a thrill of fear and excitement through her body. These were the bones of the Great Trees blazing and opening the gateway to the spirit world. The incense of their smoke filled the night. The heat pushed her back. Darkness was thrown away from the courtyard. The stones of the monastery illuminated with glowing light. Beyond them, the night hung more solidly than ever.

Time altered and stretched. The monks chanted unceasingly. At some point, the fire shrank to the height of a man. Ari Ara and the orphans crept closer as the cold began to slip in. She glanced up over the roofline. Stars shone overhead.

The oldest monks relinquished their places in the chanting. Younger monks took over. Then, unexpectedly, the chorus of voices dropped into a whisper and the sound of the Fanten drums could be heard in the distance. The Head Monk gestured for the orphans and trainees to gather closer to the fire. Ari Ara stepped into the circle with the children.

"We whisper the names because there are so many deaths in this part of Mariana's history," Head Monk explained. "This was a time when a great plague struck Mari Valley. All was nearly lost. The Fanten came down from the mountains and the mists, bearing their herbs and secrets. Out of respect for the dead and in gratitude for the Fanten's help, we whisper the names to let the ancestor spirits hear the sound of the Fanten drums. We do not know what the rhythms mean; so much of the Fanten way is cloaked in secrecy - "

"It's not a secret," Ari Ara corrected absently, half-dazed by the dance of the flames. "They would explain, but no one comes to ask or listen. That's what the Fanten Grandmother told me once."

All heads turned in her direction. She glanced up, uncomfortable to be the focus of so many curious stares.

"So, what are they drumming about?" Brol challenged her from across the circle.

Ari Ara glanced at Head Monk for permission. The whispering of names rippled all around them. The monks had split into many threads of family lines, each speaking his individual part of the recitation. The resulting sound was hair-raising and chilling. It was the only way to speak the names of the thousands lost to the plague.

Head Monk nodded for her to speak.

"It is less about the drumming than the dance," Ari Ara said slowly. "You've seen some of the Fanten dances at the villagers' spring festival, right?"

They nodded.

"There are many more - a hundred sacred dances, alone. Tonight, they dance to shake the leaves down from the lower trees - not the Great Trees, which keep their needles all year, but the trees closer to the village that bear nuts and fruits. They will dance for days or weeks to ensure that the leaves drop fully, otherwise the trees will cling to the old dry husks in the spring instead of putting their energy into fresh life."

"Superstitious nonsense," Brol muttered. A few of the trainees closest to him nodded with an air of arrogant superiority. Even Head Monk looked bemused.

Ari Ara glowered. This is why the Fanten never told the Marianans anything.

"Maybe we should dance the leaves down," Brol suggested, flapping his arms. Another trainee joined in with a mincing prance. The circle laughed.

"Do not mock what you do not understand."

Shulen's stern voice halted them mid-gesture.

"Very few lowlanders have even witnessed more than three of the Hundred Sacred Dances, none have ever lived among the Fanten, and none have learned their magic."

"Come, Shulen," Head Monk replied easily with a skeptical smile. "Surely you don't believe the folktales about Fanten magic."

"No," Shulen answer solemnly, looking down at his hands. "I only believe what I have seen with my own eyes. The Fanten use ancient magic that lowlanders have forgotten - if we ever knew it at all. They hold the mists in place around the upper rim of the mountains. They dance down the rains. They keep the Great Trees smiling benevolently upon us all."

Head Monk frowned, unconvinced.

"Eleven years ago," Shulen continued, "I was terribly wounded in a battle. The Fanten gave me back my life."

The orphans and trainees stared at him wide-eyed, knowing he was speaking about the fight to try to save Queen Alinore, when he was ripped apart and left for dead. Shulen's stony face hardened with memory.

"I will not hear the Fanten disparaged. You dishonor me if you do."

"We were just having some fun," muttered the trainee who had been mocking the dances with Brol.

Shulen stared at them with a severe gaze.

"If you are too ignorant to honor a culture, then do not shame yourself further by mocking it."

He placed a hand on Ari Ara's shoulder.

"The only one in this circle who knows any of the Sacred Dances is Ari Ara."

She blinked up at him in surprise.

"Did you not learn the common ones along with the other Fanten daughters?" he asked.

She nodded reluctantly.

"But, I am not a Fanten daughter," she began to say.

"You must have danced the autumn one with them," Shulen encouraged her.

Ari Ara shifted awkwardly.

"Well, all the girls learn this one."

"Show them," Shulen suggested, almost gently. "Teach them respect for the Fanten."

Ari Ara scowled up at him. Next time she had him alone, she decided, she would ask him exactly how he came to know so much about the elusive Fanten ways. She opened her mouth to refuse his request - but caught sight of Brol's sneering face across the circle. She glanced around. Regardless of whether they were orphans, monks, villagers, warriors, or nobles, all Marianans tended to regard the Fanten as some sort of half-civilized animal. Well, she thought, she could show them how wrong they were! The Fanten dances were far more complex and intricate than anything the Marianans knew.

Ari Ara picked her way through the orphans to an open section of the courtyard. She dropped her head, listening to the distant drums and the quiet whispers of the monks. It was odd dancing so far from the other Fanten. The dance was meant for a swirl of bodies, each tumbling over and over in the glorious cacophony of autumn. She waited for the spirit to rise within her. A Fanten never moved until the spirit arrived.

Someone snickered.

Help me, she begged the Fanten ancestors, certain they walked the mountains tonight along with all the other ghosts. *Help me,* she cried silently to any that listened in the darkness.

The flames cracked. The circle flinched. The drums thundered unexpectedly. Ari Ara glanced at the fire and heard voices on the cold breath of the wind.

Dance, young one, show them. We will dance with you.

Beyond the light of the flames and the waiting eyes of the orphans and trainees, above the chanting monks, up over the roofline of the monastery, hovering in the darkness were the forms of the Ones Who Slid Through Mist, the ancient Fanten ancestors, hundreds of them. Ari Ara saw them dancing the sacred dance, falling and tumbling in the motions of the wind-blown leaves. Like all of the Fanten daughters, she had been taught to follow the elder women and to learn the dance by mimicking their motions. And so, in Monk's Hand Monastery, she fixed her eyes on the ancient spirits and followed their lead.

She did not know that she was moving in ways that even the living Fanten across the valley did not know, learning motions from the ancestors that had been lost over the years, dancing in patterns that the Fanten dancers in the forest would give their prize sheep to see. She could not see the stunned expressions of the orphans, trainees, and monks as she danced a ritual that predated the time of the Three Brothers and harkened back to when the Great Trees and Fanten Grandmothers were sisters, bound by breath and the primordial task of turning the world through the seasons. She could not see the living humans watch her eyes trace the dances of the ancestors as her body eerily whirled and trembled with the hint of death and transformation, the closing gate of autumn and the opening door of winter. She could not see the Head Monk's mouth fall open as she shuddered in the motions of the shaking forests and rolled in the dry scrapes of leaves and branches. She could not see Shulen's expression as a hint of tears rose in the Stone One's eyes, and his lips trembled shut over memories no one knew about, memories of another time when he had watched the Fanten dancing.

She saw nothing but the ancestor spirits and the eternal movement of the dance.

CHAPTER EIGHT

. . . . .

After the dawn ritual the next morning, the monks and orphans slept. Nobstick and Teapot Monk put out bread for anyone who was hungry, then disappeared for the day. Ari Ara rattled about in the half-dazed agitation of sleeplessness. The drums of the Fanten continued to reverberate through the valley.

"Awake?"

Shulen appeared beside her. She nodded silently, staring out toward forest where the leaves still hung on the trees.

"Not yet, but soon," Shulen commented, shading his eyes from the low slant of the morning sun. "Let's go have a look," he invited.

Then he set off down the trail that snaked east from the monastery toward the Monk's Tears River.

"They're looser," he called over his shoulder. "You can hear it in how they rustle."

Ari Ara peered up at the vibrant red and orange leaves. They sounded drier as they shivered in the wind. A leaf fell. Ari Ara watched it arc slowly and gracefully earthward. She smiled, remembering a motion of the dance last night.

"Shulen," she called out, running to catch up, "how did you come to know so much about the Fanten?"

"They saved my life, and I lived with them during my recuperation. We were good friends, once."

"Once?" she asked daringly, thinking of the conversation in Head Monk's office. "Not any more?"

"We are not enemies," Shulen replied without exactly answering her question.

They were deep in the lower woods now and the canopy fluttered in a riot of color. The wind swayed the tall trees and hundreds of leaves tumbled across the glen.

"Oh!" Ari Ara gasped in appreciation.

Shulen settled against a rock and laced his fingers behind his grey hair.

"Did you know that *Azar* was once one of the Hundred Sacred Dances?" he mentioned with a yawn.

Ari Ara gaped at him.

"Oh yes, it's true," he assured her.

Shulen shut his eyes and tilted his chiseled face back into the warm sunlight, leaving her to ponder that revelation.

"Why isn't *Azar* one of the dances now?" she queried, crouching beside him.

Shulen opened one eye.

"Get from here to that rock across the glen without letting a leaf fall on you and I'll tell you," he bargained. He bit back a grin as she leapt to the challenge.

"If one lands on you, come back and start over," Shulen told her as she surveyed the pattern of falling leaves.

She gave him an exasperated look, but didn't argue. Shulen closed his eyes again, dozing lightly for a moment while listening to the quiet rustle of her step and the serious concentration of her efforts. Three times, she stopped and tromped back, kicking the dry fallen leaves in frustration. Then all fell suspiciously quiet. He opened an eye.

Ari Ara moved through the glen, sweeping between the odd patterns of the falling leaves. Shulen sat up to watch. The strange wild creature reminded him of the Fanten very much, except for the fineness of her Marianan bones and that bright red hair. If he squinted, she could be just another Fanten child amusing herself in the forest. For a moment, the past and present blurred, and he saw ghosts of the impossible. Shulen shook himself out of memories and back into the bright morning sunlight.

"Made it!" she hollered, jumping up on the stone and crowing with success. She hopped off and ran back exuberantly through the leaves, kicking them up before her. As she drew close, she scooped up an armful and tossed them on Shulen, laughing in delight. He chuckled and patted the ground beside him, indicating for her to sit.

"Well done," he commented gravely. "Although, the wind died down and gave you an easier time of it at the end."

She shrugged happily.

"Your turn," she said. "You promised to tell me."

"So I did," he mused, twirling a sculpted leaf between his fingers. "Do you want the legend or the truth?"

"Is there a difference?"

"Always," Shulen answered with a wry look. "But even more so when it comes to Fanten stories. You see, what the Fanten say is usually true, but it is rarely the whole truth or the only truth. Fanten Tongue, as you know, is filled with double meanings and metaphors. So, when it comes to an old story like this, there's a hundred truths and a thousand legends. Which do you want?"

"Both . . . or all of them," she answered promptly.

"Greedy, greedy," he teased. "Let's start with the legend. Once, a Fanten daughter fell in love with the Third Brother."

"What? *The* Third Brother?"

"Well, there's only one, otherwise there'd be a Fourth Brother."

Ari Ara smiled at the joke.

"She taught him one Fanten dance, *Azar,* the Way Between, and they danced it together like two youths at a ball in Mariana Capital. She had three children with the Third Brother and then she died."

"From what?" Ari Ara asked immediately.

"I don't know," Shulen answered thoughtfully, "but when she died, the Fanten lost *Azar* because she had not taught it to the other Fanten daughters, only to the Third Brother. He taught it to their children, who taught it to theirs, but the Fanten never re-learned it, though they had the chance, once."

"When?"

Shulen sighed as if he had known she would pry into that subject.

"I offered it back to them after they healed me, but there was not enough time . . . and other things happened."

"Like what?"

"Like a war over the Lost Heir," Shulen answered sharply.

"So, if that's the legend," Ari Ara said after a moment, "what's the truth?"

"Hmm?" Shulen replied, distracted by other thoughts.

"You said there was a legend and a truth."

"Ah yes. The truth is that the Fanten were furious at the Third Brother's wife for leaving them and so they forbade their daughters from following *Azar,* the Way Between. For it was *Azar* that opened her eyes to loving a lowlander, and *Azar* that allowed them to find their way together despite their differences, and *Azar* that mixed in the blood of their children, and yet it was *Azar* that laid her in the grave. And so, the Fanten decided not to dance it any more."

Shulen broke off. There was another part of the story, too, a version personal to him . . . one that the girl might find interesting. He glanced at the girl, expecting more of her insistent questions. However, she was dozing off, her eyes closed and her head tilting to the side. Shulen kept his silence. The rest of the story could wait. He leaned his head against the rock, slowly shutting his eyes in the warm morning light.

She woke with a sense of being watched. In the quiet way she had learned in the High Mountains, her eyes scanned the glen of trees. She saw nothing, but her intuition hinted that someone - probably Fanten - observed them from the wavering shadows and sunlight beyond the far rocks. She glanced at Shulen. His breath had fallen into the rhythm of deep rest. His chin tucked into his collarbone. His arms crossed over his chest. His eyelashes twitched in dreams.

Ari Ara rose silently and crept through the trees. Leaves fluttered down from the high branches. She peered through the trunks. A flash of motion caught the corner of her eye. Her breath paused for a moment, but she kept walking quietly in the same direction as before. Ari Ara listened for the slightest crack of twigs or rustle of dry leaves. A flock of songbirds erupted out of the low understory beneath the trees. She whirled. Her eyes scanned the woods, but saw nothing.

Ari Ara continued walking. She was certain that the observer was following her, pausing behind her and ducking out of sight when she turned. She smiled to herself, remembering old Fanten games of cat-and-mouse, slipping between shadows and trying to sneak up on the other daughters. They had an

89

uncanny knack for catching her unaware and scaring her half-to-death. Suspecting that one of them was teasing her now, she crept a fair distance from the glen, pretending to be looking ahead of her. She could just imagine the smirk on the Fanten daughter's face, arrogantly assuming Ari Ara was looking in the wrong direction. She waited until she found a perfect spot where the trees parted around a tumble of large boulders, then ducked out of sight and held her breath.

She heard the faint fall of footsteps. A twig snapped. Silence hung. Ari Ara counted to ten then leapt out from behind the huge rock.

The Fanten Grandmother perched on a boulder, chin on her hand, observing her with sharp interest.

"What are you doing here?" Ari Ara blurted out in surprise.

"What are you?" she asked back.

"I was finding out who was watching me," the girl retorted, glaring at the old woman.

"What were you doing back there in the glen?" the Fanten Grandmother demanded.

"Practicing."

"Practicing what?" the old woman questioned.

Ari Ara squirmed, thinking of what Shulen had told her about the history of *Azar*. When she did not answer, the woman stood up on the boulder and waggled a finger at her sternly.

"You did not go to the village like I told you," Fanten Grandmother chided with a frown.

"No, I went to the monastery."

"What are you learning there? Books?" she asked, chuckling over the concept.

"I'm studying with Shulen," Ari Ara said defiantly.

The Fanten Grandmother's face contorted. A fire of sharp interest flickered in her eyes. Her mouth pulled down into a scowl.

"The Stone One!" she snapped. "What's he teaching you?"

"*Azar.*"

"The Way Between!"

For a moment, Fanten Grandmother appeared shocked. Then she threw back her head and howled with laughter. In Fanten Tongue she murmured to the Great Trees in the distance. Ari Ara strained to make out her words but couldn't. The old woman wiped tears of mirth out of her eyes.

"What's so funny?" Ari Ara demanded to know.

"Fate," the silver-haired woman cackled in a mixture of annoyance and amusement. "That's what's so funny."

"I don't think so," Ari Ara grumbled.

"Neither do I," Fanten Grandmother agreed, sobering abruptly. "Training to be the Lost Heir's Champion, are you?"

She squinted suspiciously at the girl.

"Huh," Ari Ara snorted. "If there is a Lost Heir, I doubt anyone would pick me as a champion."

"Oh, there's a Lost Heir, alright," the secretive grandmother murmured with a glint in her eye.

Ari Ara leapt forward.

"Alive?"

The Fanten nodded.

"Where?!" Ari Ara asked. "How can we find the heir?"

"Follow the Stone One," Fanten Grandmother suggested wickedly.

Her peal of mocking laughter rang out. Without another word, the Fanten Grandmother darted off the rock faster than a flash of sunlight through the trees and disappeared into the shadows of the forest. Ari Ara stared at the spot where the mysterious woman had been. She kicked the dry leaves in frustration and ran back to where Shulen lay sleeping. The Fanten kept secrets better than the dead!

CHAPTER NINE

. . . . .

Follow the Stone One. The words haunted Ari Ara. She dogged Shulen's feet until he snapped at her, but learned nothing. The days shortened and the nights lengthened. A late burst of warmth struck the valley and a tide of thunderstorms swept the mountains in waves. On Old Monk Mountain, the snows gathered and melted, then vanished in a week of rains. The annual commemoration of the Battle of Shulen's Stand drew closer. The orphans and trainees whispered about it, wondering if the monks would make the usual pilgrimage over the mountain and down into the ravine to the shrine that had been built near the Queen's cave . . . but with the Great Warrior himself stalking the monastery, none dared to ask.

In the end, the warrior monks elected against the journey. The skies threatened stormy rains and when Head Monk spoke quietly to Shulen, the scarred man negated the idea with a curt shake of his head. A short and simple ceremony was held in the Main Hall as darkness fell and the winds lashed furiously across the mountains. The chants in Old Tongue sounded mournful as the approaching storm moaned outside. Shulen stood at the back, his expression harder than the stone walls of the monastery. He left immediately after the final prayers.

It was a somber and hushed evening. The senior monks snapped at the orphans for making too much noise. The trainees bickered with each other. The warrior monks moodily muttered unintelligible phrases under their breaths.

"It's strange this year with Shulen here," Minli whispered to Ari Ara. "Usually, the warrior monks retell the story of Shulen's Stand, then the trainees and some of the orphans climb over the mountain to the shrine near the Queen's cave. I've never been, not with this leg. It's a fair distance and steep going. The others always seem to have a lot of fun, half-imagining themselves in Shulen's boots, protecting the Queen, fighting . . . but with him here, it seems wrong to re-enact it blow-by-blow."

"It's too sad," Ari Ara agreed, glancing at the vacant spot where the old warrior had been standing. "Such a horrible day for him to be in Monk's Hand."

The temple bell rang and everyone quietly filed off to an uneasy slumber filled with dark dreams.

In her closet room, Ari Ara closed her eyes and tried to sleep, but the hiss of wind through the narrow gaps of the roof tiles grated on her nerves. She listened to the distant growls of thunder. Late autumn storms had none of the good humor of the summer rain showers. The cold lightning cracked with a vengeance and the thunder boomed warnings from the restless ancestor spirits. The Fanten refused to venture out on nights such as this.

Ari Ara heard Shulen's door slide open. She froze. His footsteps treaded softly past. She peered out the crack between the door and the wall. Down the corridor, midnight blue against the deeper black of night, she could see his outline . . . armed with his sword!

He slipped into the courtyard. Ari Ara thrust back her closet door and rolled out, grabbing her black shepherdess cloak and following.

Where was he going with his sword strapped to his waist? He never carried it except to practice. Ari Ara pulled the hood over her bright hair. A three quarter moon darted in and out of the furious-paced clouds. Shulen took the steps out of the monastery. She raced across the open courtyard and crouched behind the stone warrior that guarded the gateway of the buildings. He went down a dozen steps then turned to the left, taking the path to the west.

Ari Ara hesitated. He was going to the shrine, she was certain. Where else would he go on such a night? She almost turned back, but the words of the Fanten Grandmother flashed through her mind: *Follow the Stone One.*

She leapt forward. Cloaked in the black hood, she slid unseen between the shadows of night. The howl of the wind hid the sound of her footsteps. It was difficult to see Shulen, but the path was an old Fanten trail and the marks of gleaming luminescent moss and white stones could be seen even on the darkest moonless night. So long as Shulen stayed on the path, she'd have no trouble tracking him.

The journey stretched endlessly through the tumult of the wind. Ari Ara climbed the steep flank of the mountain, longing for rest, but determined to keep up with Shulen. At the crest of the Old Monk's shoulder, she ran her fingers through the air. The storm drew closer. The whispering dry wind gave way to a heavier gust, thick with moisture. She looked into the black lakes of night. The outline of the crater valley was barely visible when the moon hid behind the clouds. On the other side of the crest, an unknown landscape fell down into a sharp ravine. From the map in the Teaching Room, she knew that the cascade of mountains rose and fell toward the wide Mari River. Beyond them lay the Border Mountains and, further still, the desert. She shivered and plunged down the path.

Caution slowed her footsteps. It was easy to turn an ankle in the darkness. After a long stretch of time, Ari Ara paused to listen. Shulen still paced ahead. The wind had slowed ominously. She reached out her hand and her fingers connected with the soft hairs of a Great Tree's bark. They had descended from the higher altitudes and the forest now rose around them. The wind slowed, winding like a river through the dense solidity of the swaying trees. At the roots, the air barely moved. Ari Ara crept forward silently. In her black shepherdess cloak, she could stand right under Shulen's nose, hidden from sight, but that would not keep him from hearing a twig snapping under her foot.

Shulen also walked cautiously. He paused to listen so often that Ari Ara feared he sensed her following him. But, when he spun in a slow careful circle, she suddenly realized what he watched for. Her hair rose up on the back of her neck.

Spirits.

She cursed her own stupidity. What a fool! What was she thinking, trekking out after a warrior through an autumn storm on the anniversary of a battle? Every one of his slain enemies would be looking for him tonight. Ari Ara swallowed hard. She glanced longingly at the path back up the ravine. She took a step and something - A branch? A ghost? - snagged her hood. She clamped her hands over her scream. Shuddering, she resolutely followed Shulen. It was better to risk angry ghosts with another living human nearby. If they tried to drown her in the black river of death, she could yell for Shulen to come drag her back out. No matter what trouble she'd face for following him, it was better than death at the unseen hands.

Rain hit the tops of the Great Trees. Shulen stopped. The steep ravine leveled slightly into a small clearing. Ari Ara could not be sure, but she suspected this was Shulen's Stand. Beyond would be the slope Queen Alinore climbed, exhausted, and further still was the Fanten cave cradled in the roots of a Great Tree where her child had been born, and where she had died. The shrine stood outside the cave, according to what she had heard.

Ari Ara crouched down beside a tree, pulled her cloak tightly around her to keep out the cold, the rain, and the ghosts she uneasily sensed gathering.

Shulen stood motionless in the clearing as the past crept toward the present. Slowly, as the hiss of rain rattled the branches overhead, he drew his sword. Ari Ara shivered. Shulen moved into a fighter's stance. He lifted his head in a wordless prayer. Then, he slashed.

Ari Ara clapped her hands over her inadvertent gasp. Rain broke into full assault, lashing the forest. Ghosts leapt out of the black river of death. Lightning crashed and burst through the clearing. Shulen's face illuminated, ghastly, inhuman, twisted with pain and memories. He struck and wheeled slicing ghosts and regrets. Ari Ara wanted to shut her eyes, but could not look away. Thunder growled and Shulen's battle cry roared back. Water streamed down his face. Rain and tears beaded across his skin. He spun left and right as the ghosts of old attackers charged out of the night. He whirled in a fury of motion, closer and closer.

Ari Ara dropped to the ground. The bark of the tree split above her. Shulen spun away, his eyes lost in the past, sweeping over her, unseen. Ari Ara stayed curled tight, shaking from limb to limb. Terror clenched her muscles. Shulen staggered, reliving each wound struck in the past. The rain pounded in torrents, turning dark red with blood visions.

Ari Ara buried her face in the black wool of the cloak and silently cried to her ancestors - whoever they were - to make the nightmare stop. She wept without sound and clenched the cloak between her teeth to keep from screaming. She pleaded for the spirit of her unknown mother to come and save her.

The rain groaned and mumbled in the voices of the ancestors. The cold ground beneath her shuddered. Thunder boomed above the hissing boughs of the Great Trees.

"Enough, Shulen."

Ari Ara jolted at the sound of a woman's voice. She opened her eyes a crack.

In the clearing, the black form of a silver-lined spirit stood with her hand raised to the sharp edge of Shulen's blade. His chest heaved. His body shook. He lowered his sword.

"I failed," he murmured to the spirit. "I failed. Forgive me, please."

The woman gazed at him with tenderness. Ari Ara narrowed her eyes, trying to see more clearly. Was that Queen Alinore?

"You did all you could," she said softly.

"It was not enough."

The spirit bowed her head for a moment. The pair stood in the rain, joined in sorrow.

"I came tonight to ask - "

Shulen broke off, unable to finish.

"About the child?" the woman said.

He nodded wordlessly.

"Brave of you," the spirit answered. "To battle the ghosts of the past in hopes of finding that which was lost long ago."

Ari Ara held her breath. *Follow the Stone One*, Fanten Grandmother had told her when she asked about the Lost Heir.

"Please," Shulen said in a ragged voice.

"No, Shulen, I'm afraid not."

"Please," the warrior pleaded again, his face twisting in emotion. "I beg you."

"I cannot."

"Why not?"

"That which we hide, we rarely reveal," the spirit said, quoting an ancient Fanten saying, "not until the time is right."

The woman spoke in a tone that reminded Ari Ara so strongly of the Fanten Grandmother that she nearly jumped out of her skin. Then the woman looked directly over at Ari Ara with knowing eyes. The girl gasped soundlessly. That was *not* Queen Alinore. That was a Fanten spirit, beyond a doubt. Same eyes, same features, same haunting expression as the old Fanten Grandmother, but younger, gentler around the edges, fewer frown-lines at the corner of her mouth.

Shulen's whole body sagged in sorrow and disappointment. The woman turned back to him and her silver-edged form bent with compassion toward the man.

"I'm sorry," she said, reaching out her insubstantial hand to brush his cheek.

She began to fade back into the black river of the ancestors.

"Wait!" Shulen cried.

But she was gone.

Shulen sank to his knees in the clearing. He stared into the darkness with sightless eyes of despair. Then he bent his head into his hands and wept.

Ari Ara did not know how long she waited in the night as her heart pounded and questions raced through her mind. Who was that Fanten spirit? How did she know Shulen? What did she know about the Lost Heir? Her questions pummeled her harder than the storm that thrashed in the branches overhead. Shulen crouched in the clearing, senseless to the icy water that soaked him. The rain hissed for hours then tapered and vanished into thick mists. Sometime before dawn, Shulen rose and started up the trail to the shrine. Ari Ara rolled out from her frozen position and ran back up the shoulder of the Old Monk as fast as her stiff legs could carry her, leaving Shulen to his memories and ghosts.

CHAPTER TEN

. . . . .

The days turned cold and the nights colder still. Frost drew
its icy hand over the monastery, the forest, and the village.
Ari Ara crept with trepidation around Shulen, haunted by what
she had seen that night in the ravine. The Stone One stalked
the monastery in a dark mood. Ari Ara rose at dawn for their
training sessions cautiously and quietly. Shulen did not seem to
notice. Perhaps he enjoyed a break from her regular
impertinence. She responded to his suggestions attentively and
found his explanations offered with patience. The urge to rail
against his hard, stern ways subsided. Ari Ara didn't have the
heart for it; she had seen the Stone One cry.

The Old Monk Mountain's bald head turned white with
high altitude snows. One morning, Shulen slid back the door to
her closet room and told her to get up quickly.

"Today you learn to dodge snowflakes."

As the sky greyed over the mountains, he took her to the
small field to the east of the monastery. Ari Ara's breath hung
on the air. The clouds thickened. A few flakes tumbled from
the sky.

"Watch," Shulen said gently.

He spread his arms and waited. A tiny snowflake wafted downward. Shulen turned delicately around it as it spiraled to the ground.

Ari Ara couldn't help but smile. The Great Warrior . . . dodging snowflakes! A peal of delighted laughter rang out across the field as Shulen spun in a slow, languorous circle around the next flake. He grinned back at her and swiveled to move out of the path of another tiny white speck.

"Come, join me," he invited. "My father taught me this, long ago."

Ari Ara blinked. She could not imagine Shulen as a boy with a father who would teach him *Azar* among the swirling snow. The grey-haired Stone One wore a bittersweet expression as he reached out his hand to guide a flake to the frozen earth. He rolled over his left shoulder to avoid the next one.

Ari Ara joined him and soon discovered that it was far more difficult than Shulen made it appear. She could hardly see the tiny flakes - though they glared white against the black wool of her Fanten shepherdess cloak when they landed. The delicate lace of the snow was so lightweight that the back draft of her motions pulled the flakes toward her. They flipped and swooped in the slightest breath of air, catching her off guard. Ari Ara would have given it up for impossible if Shulen hadn't been demonstrating it beside her.

They spun slowly in the almost silent hush of snow. Shulen spoke only once.

"You must be lighter than air and twice as sensitive. Move slow, even when they fall fast."

It was strange and exhilarating. It was like the day among the leaves, but softer, subtler. She had to sense the presence of the nearly invisible flakes. At one moment, she felt the lift of the breeze and let it carry her along with the snow.

Then she saw it. The pattern snapped into alignment in her mind. Instead of moving away from the flakes, she tumbled with them, as part of them, maintaining her space within their dance, falling between them.

In the quiet, Shulen began to speak of the legends and myths of the old masters of *Azar*. There was a time when they spun through the world lighter and thicker than falling snowflakes. There were men and women, both, who could follow the Way Between with such grace and skill that they could fly on the wind and walk through walls. The followers of *Azar* danced on water and traveled through dreams. They could see into the future, turn invisible, and heal the dying with a single touch.

A true follower of *Azar*, Shulen murmured as he spun in the snow, could find the Way Between solid rock. In the driest peaks of the desert mountains, he or she could entice water to come singing out of stone.

He glanced at the child, whirling in the beauty of myths and snow, cheeks as red as her hair, blue-grey gaze seeing the masters of *Azar* in every swirl of wind. Her eyes shone with the stories of ancient times. Ari Ara's grin curled across her face. A crack split in the Stone One, hair-thin, but irreparable. Without knowing it, she had found the Way Between the hard armor of Shulen's heart.

The snow thickened. The wind kicked up. In seconds, both she and Shulen were covered with flakes. The temple bell rang out.

"Good work, kitten," Shulen commented as they walked back down to the monastery. He let his hand fall on her head, giving her a pat of approval. "Even Emir Miresh never mastered the art of dancing the Way Between the Snow."

Over the next week, the winter tumbled in quickly and snow piled up in the courtyard. One day, after lunch, Minli grabbed her by the hand.

"Come on!" he shouted.

Hauling her behind him, he crowded around Second Monk in the midst of the excitedly shrieking orphans. He waved his hand wildly over his head.

"Now, Minli, you know - "

"She'll shovel with me," Minli interrupted with a gleam in his eyes. "Please?" he begged. Second Monk relented and passed a wooden sled out of the side closet to the boy. Ari Ara's eyes grew round. Minli maneuvered past the other orphans. He hauled the sled by its rope and pointed to the pile of shovels that leaned next to the Main Hall.

"Get two," he said, "and meet me at the top of the stairs."

Nervous excitement sent her racing. She returned with the shovels slung over her shoulder. Minli was already sitting on the sled, leg tucked under the front, hands clasping the rope.

"Sit behind me and hold on. Lean right to turn right, lean left for the other direction. Stick the shovels next to my crutch."

It was crazy. It was dangerous. She leapt forward with excitement.

"We're going to kill ourselves," she muttered, peering over the edge of the stairs.

"There's a trail, see?" Minli said, pointing off to the side where a half-buried indent in the snow wound down the slope. "It's too dangerous to go straight down the steps. It's safer down the side trail, but we still have to make the turns correctly. Here, practice a moment."

Minli showed her how to bank, leaning left, then right.

"Ready?"

She gulped. She had seen the orphans flying down the hill from a distance, but it looked a lot steeper now that she was sitting perched at the top, mere seconds from hurtling down.

"Ari Ara?" he asked again.

"Yes! Go!" she shouted before she lost her nerve.

"Push!" he ordered, dropping the rope over his knees and shoving at the snow with his hands.

She joined him, jostling her weight forward to help pick up momentum. They creaked over the lip of the trail, Minli's end of the sled tipped forward . . . and off they flew! Powdery snow billowed around them. Cold air howled past her ears. Ari Ara felt a scream in her lungs and turned it into a whoop of delight at the last second.

"Left!" Minli yelled.

She leaned. They turned.

"Right!" he called again.

They flung their bodies the opposite direction.

Wild with excitement, Ari Ara let out a Fanten trill. As they raced down a straight section, she released one clenched hand from the back of Minli's jacket and threw it up in the air.

"We're flying!!!" she hollered.

She felt his laughter in front of her.

"Right!" he warned her.

She shifted. The speed of the turn tilted them up the bank in a breathless arc. They straightened and hurtled down the next section.

"On the count of three, roll left!" Minli yelled suddenly.

"What?!" she yelped.

"It's the end, I forgot to tell you - one, two, three!"

She dove left. Minli followed. The empty sled crashed into the mound of snow set up to stop them. They rolled onto their backs, laughing breathlessly.

They scrambled out of the way of the next sled speeding down the trail. Ari Ara waded through the knee-deep snow to grab their sled, shovels, and his crutch.

"Now," Minli informed her, "we shovel our way back up."

She groaned, looking at the long submerged staircase.

"But," he added with a grin, "we can take breaks and sled for a while."

Ari Ara cheered. She grabbed a shovel.

"Let's go!"

The days grew startlingly short. The nights stretched deep and long. The villagers barely stirred from their squat thatched houses. The Fanten were not seen at all. Ari Ara often paused under the overhangs of the courtyard, bundled in the impenetrable felt of her shepherdess cloak, watching the swirling snow.

A curl of delight spread across her features as she thought of the hot stone fires waiting in the Main Hall. She never knew winter could be so wonderful - full of shivery time outdoors interspersed by long hours by the glowing warmth that burned from the black stones the monks acquired from the miners. The villagers burned mixtures of deadwood and dried dung. The scent of the smoke drifted east with the winds most of the time. The Fanten forbade anyone in the crater valley of Monk's Hand to cut down trees for burning. They, themselves, retreated underground for the winter, semi-hibernating in the deep caverns that lay between the roots of the Great Trees.

Some days, when the monastery clanged with the pent-up noise of so many people, Ari Ara felt a twinge of longing for the hushed quiet of the sleeping Fanten winters . . . until she remembered the long hours of darkness and boredom, hunger and chill. She had never told anyone about her early years with the Fanten, and how they surrendered into a deep trance during the cold months. They had gathered food for her and lectured her not to wake them, not to disturb the elders, and not to ask too many questions. They told her that her bloodlines were too fitful and restless to sleep the Fanten sleep.

"How did I survive as a baby, then?" she had asked once.

"Some of us stayed awake," one of the women answered so sourly that Ari Ara didn't dare ask more questions.

She found it odd, then, that as winter deepened she longed for rest. At dawn, she resented the early morning sessions with Shulen; her limbs felt heavy and sluggish. After a few days, Shulen switched their schedule, practicing with her at midday when the trainees took their lunch break. By evening chants, she would doze off in the middle of chores and pick at her food while the orphans made fun of her sleepiness. *Ari Ara*, she sighed, *not this, not that.* Too loud for Fanten; too quiet for Marianans.

The last week before solstice, the children began to ricochet off the walls of the monastery, exuberantly loud and increasingly festive. Even the usual solemnity of the senior monks was disturbed by the antics.

"What's got into them?" Ari Ara asked Minli as a pair of six-year-olds darted past shrieking at the top of their lungs.

"Feast Days," Minli answered absently.

The Feast Days of the Three Brothers came right around winter solstice: the eldest first, Marin's Day; the second on solstice, Shirar's Day, and the third day was Alaren's Day. Ari Ara had seen the activities in the village last winter. The festive air of the Feast Days had seemed lonesome to her as the families herded together and everyone forgot her existence. There were presents and games, no lessons or chores, and a huge celebration in the village center on Marin's Day. The children frequented the bakers' stalls for sweet rolls and dumpling stew and spice cakes. Ribbons and wreathes hung over every doorway.

"Will the monastery go down to the village this year?" Ari Ara asked, vaguely recalling the sight of grey-robed monks last year.

"Yes," Minli's eyes glazed over in remembered rapture as he explained. "We always go to the village dances and take part in the huge game of Catch the King with puppets of Marin and Shirar. The orphans all join in the village-wide Search for the Lost Heir. It's different than our version; they use a hidden doll and it carries a bundle stuffed with candies and surprises. Don't the Fanten celebrate the Feast Days?"

"No," she answered. *They were all asleep.* "Those are Marianan and Desert traditions, not Fanten."

"Too bad, then. You missed out on a lot of fun all these years," Minli commented.

As the Feast Days approached, she had to agree. The monastery had its traditions, too. The monks were full of old stories and folk tales. Work stopped for large parts of the day while the senior monks told tale after tale about Marin and Shirar. There were hardly any stories about the Third Brother, Alaren, and those that existed were eerie cautionary tales about meddling in other people's business.

"Those aren't true stories," Shulen warned Ari Ara in an undertone one evening. "Marianans wouldn't know a true story about the Third Brother if it smacked them in the face. They make him into a meddling fool to undermine his power."

"Do you know the true stories?" she whispered back.

Shulen did not answer. He glowered at the senior monks before turning on his heel and leaving. Ari Ara shrugged. Shulen was in a grumpy mood because the trainees were losing their concentration. His practice session with them this morning had devolved into a snowball fight.

The entire monastery echoed with laughter, high-spirited pranks, and chatter. Ari Ara perched by the door to the Main Hall watching everything. She loved the ballads the senior monks broke into in the evenings. Her favorites were the ancient songs in Old Tongue, but there were also songs that every monk, trainee, and orphan knew, and the sound of over one hundred people joyously singing together moved her to inexplicable tears. The Fanten didn't sing - at least, she had never heard them - and she had never tried. Quietly, tentatively, she hummed along, enjoying the sensation of sound reverberating in her chest.

On the morning of Marin's Feast Day, Shulen called her into his room. Certain that she was in trouble, Ari Ara shuffled her feet, stalling for time as she tried to remember what she had - or hadn't - done in the past week.

"There's a Feast in the village today," Shulen began as she entered the room. "You can't go - "

"What?!" she yelped, horrified.

"- looking like last year's bedraggled scarecrow," he finished.

Shulen gestured to the trunk in the corner of the room. On top lay a pair of trousers, a blue tunic, a woven belt, and a garment that literally took her breath away: a gleaming black cloak of fine Fanten wool with a single silver band from an elder sheep's fleece, woven in an intricate pattern, subtle and elegant.

"Are they for me?" she cried in an awed voice.

"Well, they're not going to fit me," Shulen replied wryly.

Ari Ara ran to gather them up, her fingers stroking the woven cloak reverently.

"Fanten wool," she breathed.

"Woven in Mariana patterns," Shulen explained. "An *Ari Ara* cloak, not this, not that, but perhaps something that surprises us all."

She held it up with a look of sheer wonder.

"No one has ever given me a gift before - not like this. Only patched old things from the Fanten sisters."

Ari Ara touched the freshly made trousers and the bright blue of the tunic. The belt was stiff from the loom, unbent.

"Hurry up and get ready," Shulen said in a gruff voice that fooled no one.

Ari Ara spun and flung her arms around Shulen's waist in gratitude. Before he could react, she whirled again, gathered the clothes, and disappeared out the door with a yelp of delight.

"You'd think you'd given her a ball gown," Second Monk commented in amusement to Shulen as they descended the long carved steps down from the monastery to the village. Ari Ara walked a stone's throw ahead, absorbed in her own world, stroking the edge of the woven cloak as if checking to make sure it was real. The snowy slopes echoed the sounds of festive voices. The orphans shoved each other in the drifts and threw snowballs. The trainees skidded and slid down the icy patches, whooping and hollering. The senior monks cautiously picked their way down the steps, patiently attended by the warrior monks.

Shulen nodded silently. Inwardly, his heart was both pleased and sober. As he looked over the bowl of Monk's Hand, he wondered what sort of a world his generation had wrought that a child could grow up ungifted and ignored. He cursed the wars that turned sons and daughters into lonely orphans, and then trained them into warriors.

"All the orphans will have gifts tonight, but none quite so fine," Second Monk mentioned to Shulen, acknowledging the kindness of the old warrior's gift to his apprentice.

Shulen sighed. Whole societies of women in Mariana Capital put together endless rounds of charitable events to fundraise for gifts for the orphans on the Feast Days. Half of Mariana's social season was made up of these lavish affairs as the nobles assuaged their guilt by drinking wine and collecting trinkets for the orphans.

"There's no substitute for peace and parents," Shulen murmured quietly.

Second Monk turned to look questioningly at him, but he said nothing more. Ahead of them, the wiry girl leapt the steps two at a time.

Ari Ara entered the village with her head lifted high, feeling equal to the Lost Heir or the Champion. She nodded to the cobbler's wife. She lifted her hand in greeting to the cattle herder's passel of children, but did not run after them to see what mischief they were brewing. Ari Ara was determined to behave today and make Shulen proud. Everyone would know her cloak, tunic, trousers, and belt came from Mariana Capital; there was nothing like them in Monk's Hand. As his apprentice, her conduct would reflect on his honor - for better or for worse.

When the tanner complemented her on her attire, she met his eye and said thank you with such dignity that he stood for a long moment after she passed, wondering if this was the same redheaded shepherdess that had been running through Monk's Hand for years.

"Will you look at that one," he muttered to his wife. "I heard tell she's training under the Stone One."

"Done some good, it seems," the woman replied.

"Aye. Nearly didn't recognize her in all that finery."

"Or all those *manners*," his wife corrected drolly, watching the usually wild child pause to speak respectfully with a circle of old weaver women asking to see her cloak. Ari Ara even unwrapped it from her shoulders and held it out for them to examine the craftsmanship more closely.

"Well, it'd take the Stone One to tame her," the tanner sighed.

"Tame?" his wife exclaimed, huffing. "You can put a fine saddle blanket on a desert horse, but that don't mean the devil beast is tame!"

He shared a laugh over the jibe, but cast another glance at the fiery red of the girl's hair and suspected that nothing would ever get that hint of the Desert People's madness out of the girl's blood. Pity that. If anyone could temper it, he supposed, it would be the Stone One.

Ari Ara tossed the end of her cloak over her shoulder Fanten style as the first chords of music leapt out of the square. Where was Minli? She wove through the crowd, trying to find him. He wasn't near the stage, nor the market aisle, nor down in front with the other orphans. He would have come early, she was sure, to give him time with his leg. She circled back through the empty streets, searching.

A squawk of crows caught her attention, and she veered toward the noise, wondering what brought them down so close to all the bustle. It wasn't like the crows; they'd rather swoop in when they thought no one was watching, not amidst all this commotion. Their chatter sounded strangely distorted. A piping yelp shot out above the cawing.

Ari Ara burst into a run. She knew that sound.

CHAPTER ELEVEN

. . . . .

Ari Ara skidded around a corner and bolted up a side street, slipping on a patch of ice and scrambling back onto her feet.

At the end of the winding street, she saw them. A pack of village lads circled Minli in a ring, cawing and squawking as he hopped awkwardly on his one foot. They mocked his black orphan's robes and flapped their arms at him, teasing him for looking like a small crow. His eyes were red and shiny. A taller youth stood back slightly, holding his crutch and smirking.

Brol.

Ari Ara's dislike flared into hatred.

"Leave him alone!" she shouted, racing toward the circle and grabbing the crutch with both hands. "You give that back, Brol!"

"Oh look, the Wild Howler of the mountains has come to rescue you," Brol sneered. The other boys laughed. Brol kicked at her shins, but she jumped his foot and tugged at the crutch while he stood unbalanced. He teetered and she wrenched it from his grasp.

"Here," she murmured to Minli, handing it to him.

113

"Look who thinks she's the Heir's Champion, all dressed up high and mighty," one of the village boys called out, his eyes narrowing at her tunic and cloak.

"He might be the Lost Heir for all you know," Ari Ara retorted. "So leave him alone."

The circle broke into a riot of laughter at the notion.

"A cripple and a creature?" Brol mocked. "Heir and Champion?"

The laughter exploded even harder.

"Come on," Ari Ara muttered to Minli, "let's get out of here."

She started to leave, but two tall boys blocked her, shoving her backward.

"Not so fast, desert demon," Brol hissed coldly, drawing closer. "If he's the Heir and you're the Champion, you have to defend his honor before you leave."

The village lads chuckled in anticipation. Ari Ara scowled. It was an old village game - Heir and Champion - used in everything from skirmishes to marbles to walking fences to footraces. The adults used it in drinking and gambling games where one's best friend had to defend your honor and pay your debts.

The ring closed tight around them. The village boys cracked their knuckles. Ari Ara's eyes darted across the faces, noting several who already held grudges against her.

"Fine," she spat back.

"Ari, no -" Minli protested.

"But, you let him out of the circle, according to the rules. Whether I best you or you best me, he walks out unharmed. Deal?"

"Fair enough, desert demon," Brol agreed. His eyes narrowed with eagerness for the fight. With one hand, he grabbed Minli by the jacket and shoved him out of the circle. Then he pointed to one of the boys. "Guard him. Make sure he doesn't go running for adults."

"Yeah," Ari Ara scoffed, "because that would ruin everything, having to mess with a real fighter like Shulen, rather than a half-sized girl who - "

She broke off as he lunged, dodging swiftly. The village boys jumped in. A storm of surging fists and hurling kicks broke out. Ari Ara had a moment of panic - she'd never studied the Way Between a Horde of Angry Wasps! A blow stung across the side of her skull. A fist hit her eye. Something cracked across her nose. Frantic, she dove away and rolled, leaping back to her feet only to avoid another fist. Someone's grip tried to pin her arms. She twisted. Her beautiful cloak tore off with a ripping sound. She slipped free and whirled out of reach of the next attack.

Distantly, she heard Minli cry out. She glanced to see - and a blow cracked into her ribs. Gasping, she reeled. Brol had Minli's crutch again and he swung it hard at her head. She ducked. He swung again, faster than she could leap aside, so she grabbed it with both hands in a smack that shot stabbing pain up her arms. She gripped it with sheer determination and hauled backwards, dragging Brol off balance. She pulled him in a circle as he struggled for his footing, using his body to clear the others back a pace.

"Why not fight me like a man?" she challenged him. "One on one - "

He dug his heels in and yanked the crutch. She was hauled off her feet and spun in a circle. She heard the others laughing and could only imagine how ridiculous she looked, being flung full-bodied through the air. With a heave that sent a jolt through her aching ribs, she wrenched her body upwards, locking her legs around the wooden pole. The sudden shift of weight pulled the crutch from Brol's grip and she fell hard onto the cold frozen ground. She rolled as he dove at her, throwing her hands up around her head to protect it.

"Enough!"

Shulen's voice cracked through the fight. Ari Ara froze instantly. Brol's foot smashed into her side. She cried out.

"I said, enough."

Dimly, she saw Shulen haul Brol backward by the collar of his shirt as the village boys scattered and ran off.

"Get to your feet," he told Ari Ara in a voice colder than ice.

"But," she gasped, coughing out bits of dirt and straw.

"Get up."

Grimacing, she staggered to standing. One hand clutched her ribs. Her tunic was torn. Her cloak lay ripped and crumpled off to the side. Her nose was bleeding. Her lip stung where it had split and her eye was half-blind with swelling from a blow she couldn't even remember.

"Apologize," Shulen growled.

"I didn't - " Brol began.

"Not you," the grey-haired Stone One snapped with undisguised scorn. "Her."

Ari Ara's mouth fell open.

"It's not her fault!" Minli cried.

"I'm not listening to excuses or explanations," Shulen stated sharply. "A follower of *Azar* never brawls in the street like a common pig herder."

The harsh tone of his disappointment stung worse than her split lip.

"He," Shulen went on, scathingly, "may have been brought up to think that picking on the seemingly defenseless proves one's manhood . . . "

Ari Ara saw Brol's face close in dark fury. Shulen utterly ignored him as he continued to ream out his apprentice.

" . . . but you are under my instruction, and I have higher standards for you than this despicable scuffle. Apologize."

She stared at Shulen in disbelief.

"Now!" he ordered.

Ari Ara gritted her teeth over pain and injustice. Her head reeled.

"I apologize - "

She meant to say, *for descending to your pathetic level*, but a blackness rose in her eyes, the world spun, and her legs crumbled out from under her.

CHAPTER TWELVE

. . . . .

Words rolled like garbled waves.

" . . . could have done serious harm."

" . . . and what do you call this? A slight scrape?"

"She has to learn . . . "

" . . . from what I hear, she was sufficiently provoked . . . "

"You or I would have avoided that fight."

That was Shulen, she thought dimly.

"You and I are not children."

Second Monk's voice was sticking up for her. The very idea stunned her, though she could not react. Her whole body felt pinned in thick mud. Everything hurt.

"She has to learn how to avoid fights, not just fists," Shulen argued.

"Humph," Second Monk snorted. "At least until she's grown closer to her opponent's size."

They laughed, softly, ruefully.

"It was . . . " Shulen paused, seeking words. "It was like watching Miresh at that age, but perhaps even more startling."

"Because of *Azar*?"

"Yes. Because she did not - not once - strike back. She neither backed down, nor ran away, nor struck at them. And had she been a year older or a head taller or fifty pounds heavier . . . I think she would have dispersed them long before I arrived."

"I wish I had seen it," Second Monk commented.

"Be glad you didn't," Shulen replied sharply. "Our little kitten was being torn apart by a pack of dogs. It was commendable, but doomed. "

There was nothing commendable about it, in her estimation. She recalled evading more fists than she ever hoped to see again in her life, desperately trying to get out of a losing situation.

She heard the door slide to the side as Second Monk left.

She groaned and her eyes fluttered open. The room spun.

"Awake, then?" Shulen said in a gentle voice, coming to kneel beside her cot. She was in the small sitting room of his quarters. A cot had been set up along the sidewall.

"You're not mad at me?" she croaked.

"Oh yes, I am. Furious," he said in amusement. "You should have been able to avoid at least half of the blows that lodged in your ribs."

"I tried," she said in a pathetic voice.

"I know," Shulen said kindly.

"Minli?"

"He's fine."

"Brol?"

"Has been strongly reprimanded by the Head Monk," Shulen answered. Seeing her scowl, he added, "He has been ordered out of trainings for three months, assigned other duties, and will not stand Trials in the spring."

Ari Ara's eyes widened at the news. He deserved it, she thought furiously, for picking on Minli, fighting dirty, and ripping her -

"My cloak!" she cried, remembering. "It's ruined."

"Not ruined, kitten. Just a little battered, like you."

He reached to the small shelf beside him and pulled it out. The cloak unfurled as he handed it to her. She saw that the long tear had been carefully mended.

"Who fixed it?" she asked, grateful for the effort.

"I did."

Ari Ara blinked. It was impossible to imagine the grey-haired warrior sewing with a thin needle and thread.

"Anyone who dodges swords for a profession ought to be able to mend the inevitable rips and tears. If only the human body could be repaired as easily . . . or the heart, which is the most difficult of all to mend."

Shulen looked questioningly at her.

"Can you sit up?"

Gingerly, she tried. The room lurched wildly then stayed put. Shulen poured her a cup of tea and passed it to her. She gulped it down, suddenly parched.

"Tell me what happened, step by step," Shulen said. "We'll review it like a sparring match and learn from it."

So, she related all that had happened from hearing the teasing crow calls to Shulen's arrival. Here and there, he stopped her to point out how she could have done differently or avoided a blow. Finally, he sat back and asked,

"If you could change one moment, or one single move, what would it be?"

Ari Ara thought about it. The room fell into an easy quiet as he waited.

"When Brol teased us for thinking we were the Champion and Lost Heir," she said finally, "I could have just agreed that it was ridiculous, then he wouldn't have had anything to fight me over. That was the Way Between, and I missed it."

Shulen looked at her approvingly.

"It's time for this, I think," he said, reaching toward the small shelf of his belongings. He pulled down a weathered book. "And, it is appropriate timing, since today is the Feast Day of Alaren."

Shulen chuckled at her startled expression.

"You've been out cold for some time. Second Monk was quite concerned."

"But not you?" Ari Ara questioned, raising her eyebrow.

"I know your head's harder than it looks."

He laughed at her expression then glanced down at the book in his hands as if uncertain. His eyes clouded for a moment before he shook whatever haunted him out of his mind.

"This is a gift. It was my father's and his father's before that. I had hoped to give it to my - " he broke off then continued. "Well, no matter. It's for you. Please take care of it. There are only a few copies in existence."

"What is it?" Ari Ara asked, hoping he wouldn't make her read it.

"Stories of the Third Brother's Way," Shulen read from the front cover. "Emir Miresh read it while he was recuperating from a particularly painful bout of hardheaded stupidity, as I did before him. Now, it's your turn."

He handed it to Ari Ara who held it gingerly as if it would either break or bite. She cautiously flipped through the pages. The complicated characters inside taunted her ignorance.

"Uh, thank you," she said after a moment, already scheming ways to trick Minli into reading it and telling her the stories.

"It contains tales of verbal and mental *Azar* . . . the inner work of the Way Between," Shulen explained. "Long before a physical fight, *Azar* provides a Way Between the rising conflict, an approach that allows us to de-escalate hostilities and to address the underlying issues leading us into a fight."

He studied the book in her hands.

"It is far more difficult to master than physical, outer *Azar*," he warned her. "I, myself, am only a student of it."

Ari Ara groaned. If Shulen couldn't do it, she didn't stand a chance. She couldn't even read the characters on the cover.

Shulen must have had similar doubts because he added; "I ought to have started you out with the Third Brother's book. Despite all your speed and agility on foot, you have little aptitude for ending disputes and avoiding trouble."

He raised one of his grey eyebrows at her as she sighed.

"It's my desert demon temper," she muttered, thinking of Brol's taunts.

"Who told you that?" Shulen asked carefully, putting the kettle back on the hot coals in the fireplace to warm.

"Everybody says so," Ari Ara mumbled, avoiding his eyes. "It's in my fire hair and my blood."

Shulen said nothing for a moment, watching the steam slide out of the mouth of the kettle.

"You shouldn't listen to what Marianans say about Desert People," he warned her solemnly. "You'd do better to wait until you meet some yourself."

Ari Ara rolled her eyes. That wasn't likely to happen in this lifetime.

"Desert People have a great passion for life and high spirits," Shulen commented. "When provoked, they will fight

123

ferociously, but they, far more so than Marianans, strive to master their tempers. If you do have Desert blood, it is an honor to you . . . and it also demands that you control your fire with the same skill as the Desert King."

"The Desert King?" Ari Ara blurted out. "But, he started so many wars!"

Shulen frowned at her.

"You live on the Marianan side of this story . . . be careful about believing everything you are told."

He poured the last round of tea out of the pot. Ari Ara decided to say nothing more.

CHAPTER THIRTEEN

. . . . .

Her ribs ached and her head throbbed, but that didn't get her out of kitchen duties. The next day, Ari Ara sat near the window, watching the afternoon practice in the cold, cleared-off courtyard while she peeled apples for Teapot Monk.

Outside, the trainees' breaths rose on the frigid air in plumes of white smoke. Exertion kept them warm against the snow. Their cheeks turned bright red as they worked. Ari Ara stretched her sore back and winced as her ribs creaked in reply. She picked up another apple, sourly frowning at the heap of fruit. Her hands kept falling idle. The boys had been practicing kicks and dodges all afternoon. They seemed to prefer kicking to dodging - which seemed backwards to her.

Minli plopped down beside her and began to help peel the apples.

Shulen whistled through his fingers. The sparring halted. The youth gathered to listen to his comments, crouching and panting from the challenging drill. He demonstrated a nuance to the younger boys then made them repeat it.

"He's a good teacher," Minli said quietly. "Patient."

Ari Ara turned to her friend.

"Minli, did you ever want . . . " she trailed off, avoiding his eyes as she tilted her head in the direction of the practice in the courtyard.

"Of course," he answered in a low voice. His eyes gleamed with yearning. He blushed and glanced away. "But, it's not possible with this." He gestured to his leg. "No one even bothered to ask me before."

"I'll teach you," Ari Ara offered. "Not *Attar* - I can't do that - but I could teach you some of what I'm learning in *Azar*."

"I thought it was supposed to be a secret," Minli pointed out in a hushed tone.

Instinctively, they both glanced over their shoulders to see if the kitchen monks were nearby. They ducked their heads closer together.

"Yeah, but who cares?" Ari Ara answered. "It's stupid to just have a few people know it. What if a plague strikes us all dead in one day? Besides, you could have used it in the village, and I could have used some back up," she admitted, pointing to her bruises.

Minli sighed.

"There's no point, not with my leg."

"Nonsense," Ari Ara replied swiftly. "Remember how Shulen made me stand on one foot all day?"

Minli giggled.

"You nearly stayed there all night."

She chucked an apple peel at his chest.

"Well, you've been standing on one foot for years," she pointed out. "You ought to be studying *Azar*. That way, you wouldn't need a champion. You'd be one."

Minli stared at his leg, uncertain.

"Besides," she threw in casually, as if she hadn't spent all night scheming up this conversation, "Shulen gave me a book on inner *Azar* . . . you can teach me to read it."

Minli grinned.

"I was wondering when you'd 'fess up," he needled her in good humor.

"How long have you known?" she demanded.

"Since the day you claimed you'd die of boredom to get out of admitting you couldn't read."

"And you never said anything?!"

"We're friends, right?"

Ari Ara gave him a grateful look.

"So it's a deal?" she asked, sticking out her hand.

Minli nodded.

"Deal," he agreed.

They shook and sealed the bargain.

That evening, they hid in a back storeroom after dinner. The underground room was carved into the solid rock of the mountain. It was quiet and cool; they wore their cloaks to keep off the chill. The lamp fought to push back the shadows.

"Here," she said, shoving the small, thick book at him.

Minli whistled appreciatively.

"Do you know how rare this is?"

"Shulen mentioned something about it," she answered with a shrug.

"There are exactly five copies. Four are in the Capital Library. I never heard where the fifth one went."

"Apparently, Shulen's father's father had it. Emir Miresh read it."

"This copy?!" Minli said excitedly, holding the volume reverently.

Ari Ara nodded.

"Yes, he'd gotten himself beat up and Shulen made him read it while recuperating."

They sat down on a stack of grain sacks. Minli pointed to the cover.

"Let's start with these three characters - *Stories of the Third Brother's Way*."

"That's more words than characters," Ari Ara pointed out.

"Yes. A character is a picture of an idea. See? This one is stories, with a little tail stroke connecting it to the next character to say whose stories - the Third Brother's. The actual symbol is a stylized portrait of Alaren, see? The last character is the sign for *Azar*."

"What's this?" she questioned, pointing to a symbol imprinted on the leather cover.

"That's just an illustration," Minli said. "See how it's different from the brushstrokes?"

Ari Ara squinted at it and eventually agreed that it wasn't painted with ink and brush, nor did it sweep with the same lines as the other characters. It was solid and round with two sets of patterns covering half of each side. She shrugged. Mysteries.

"So," she asked, turning back to the inner pages of the book, "if that one's *Azar* . . . does that mean *Attar* and *Anar* have their own characters?"

"Yes, here." Minli slid off the stack of sacks onto the dusty floor and drew them in a pile of spilled flour. Ari Ara quickly crouched down beside him. The signs were similar, a triad of related ideas.

"And this is Alaren, Marin, and Shirar," Minli said, drawing them. "See how Alaren is akin to the other two brothers?"

"How am I going to remember all this?" Ari Ara demanded.

"Practice," Minli answered pragmatically. Then he grinned. "Wait until you learn Desert Tongue. It's all by sound . . . each sound makes a letter, the letters form words."

"But that's completely different than Marianan!" Ari Ara protested.

"Yeah, the descendants of Marin and Shirar fought a whole war over it," Minli said, shaking his head at the stupidity.

"How do I write Ari Ara?" she asked, curious.

Minli laughed.

"That's an interesting question, actually. There's several ways. Here's how you would write it in Desert Tongue, just as it sounds *Ar-i Ar-a*." Minli drew it as he spoke. "And here it is in Marianan . . . see? Those are the two characters for *Not this, Not that*."

Ari Ara frowned. There was something achingly familiar about the strokes. Those firm diagonal slashes of negation had been slicing through her life as long as she could remember.

"Is there another option?"

Minli nodded.

"There's the Old Tongue version. It's . . . it's more poetic, in a way."

He drew a symbol in the spilled flour on the floor, swirling a graceful sweep of his finger into a circle that nearly closed but instead ended with a dot on one end.

"This character doesn't mean *Not this, Not that*," he explained. "It means all the things not yet defined or known. We don't have a word for it in Marianan, not exactly, so we just use the symbol in Old Tongue, *Ari Ara*, for the sense of the possibility that lies between."

"The possibility that lies between," Ari Ara echoed. "I like that. No one ever explained my name that way before."

129

Minli heard a funny catch in her voice, as if she were about to cry.

"Well, for someone who follows the Way Between, it's fitting, isn't it?"

Ari Ara nodded. With a sense of wonder, she reached out her hand and drew her name.

Between chores and lessons, Ari Ara was more often than not seen bent over the book, lips moving silently, finger tracing the characters across the page. She dodged out of chores more than ever, disappeared before anyone could wrangle her into duties, and hid in obscure corners of the monastery to scour the pages in the semi-darkness. Reading was an infuriatingly slow process for a girl accustomed to racing the wind across the High Mountains. If her ribs had not ached so painfully, Ari Ara would have given up on reading long ago, dropping the book in favor of dancing and spinning through the motions of *Azar*. But, she was forced to sit still during the short days and long nights, so she persevered, plodding her way through memorizing characters and trying to recognize them on the page. She worked over each line a hundred times, deciphering the meaning. By the time she turned a page, she would be trembling with the exertion of concentration, her forehead aching from her determined scowl.

Any chance they had, Minli would teach her the meanings of new characters. With each one, obscure lines would suddenly illuminate in her comprehension like dawn light sliding over the High Mountains.

"What's this one?" she asked.

"Blacksmith," he answered.

And the page suddenly erupted into meaning. She saw the character of Alaren walking through the looming threat of war, talking one blacksmith after another into refusing to forge weapons. The characters turned into pictures and the story played out in front of her eyes. She saw Alaren - who she imagined looking something like Shulen, grey and ancient - and the blacksmiths standing firm against the fury of the warring brothers, refusing to send the sons and daughters of both nations into battle, rounding up the swords and spears, and hammering them back into ploughs and rakes.

"That's why the trainees study weaponless fighting," Minli pointed out. "Because, once, the blacksmiths refused to make weapons."

"Wish they still did that," Ari Ara grumbled. "We might still have parents."

Minli borrowed the book one night and came to class the next day with his head buzzing with Third Brother stories. His eyes glazed over during the lesson - a dull memorization of the dates of various political edicts - until Scholar Monk chastised him for his lack of concentration and ordered him to copy scrolls all evening as punishment.

Ari Ara snuck into the copy room after supper to keep him company.

"Don't distract me or I'll never finish," he warned her miserably as she slid the book onto the table next to him.

"Just tell me what you read that was so good," she begged.

He pointed it out. Their heads bent over the table. Silence fell, broken only by the faint sound of the brush and the turn of the page.

Ari Ara burst out laughing.

"You were imagining yourself as the Third Brother, weren't you? That's why you were so distracted in class. Come on, admit it!"

He swiped the brush at her to stop her teasing and nearly upset the inkbottle.

"Well, yeah, wouldn't you?" he confessed, blushing. "There he was with a broken leg, the bandits surrounding him, a sword at his throat - "

" - and they spared his life because he told them that he was a historian who wanted to write down their stories," Ari Ara finished, laughing heartily at Alaren's audacity.

"Wait until you read the next story," Minli enthused. "You'll see how that encounter leads into him negotiating a treaty with the bandits to get them to stop raiding the villages."

"How?" she demanded.

But Minli wouldn't tell. She had to painstakingly decipher each character to learn how Alaren listened to the maligned bandits and discovered how the laws had forced them to starve in poverty, hang for crimes of petty theft, or run into the hills to be bandits. Ari Ara read about how Alaren brokered an agreement between them and the local soldiers. The bandits "surrendered" their thieving way of life in exchange for the chance to build a village for their families and to establish trades and farms. Then Alaren went to his brother, King Marin, and worked to change the death laws that were driving people into desperation.

The story went on, but Ari Ara's eyes grew heavy. She leaned her head on her arms and drifted into dreams where she traveled with Alaren on his adventures. The temple bell boomed and woke her.

"Wake up!" Minli shook her. "We fell asleep."

Stiff and aching from sleeping in the copy room, they hurried off to start the day.

After breakfast, Ari Ara hid the book under her tunic and snuck it into class. When Scholar Monk was busy writing on the board, she opened the book surreptitiously and picked up where she had left off in the Third Brother's story. Scholar Monk assigned them a treatise on the ten proper ways to translate Old Tongue into modern Marianan. She ignored the assignment and read the book under her parchment. Alaren had gathered the bandits, police, villagers, and nobles for . . . what? Her mind hit a blank wall.

"Minli," she hissed, leaning across the aisle. "What's this character?"

He glanced toward Scholar Monk before whispering back.

"A truth-telling assembly. Alaren gathered everyone to tell their side of the story to help prevent the same thing from happening again."

"What are you two whispering about?" Scholar Monk scolded with a frown.

"Uh . . . the third way to transcribe Old Tongue," Ari Ara answered quickly, shoving the book out of sight. "I, um, had a question about the shape of the strokes in modern Mari -"

"That's the sixth way that deals with adaptations of strokes," Scholar Monk said crossly. Ari Ara nodded with what she hoped was an appreciative expression before turning back to the stories under her parchment. She read about how the truth-telling fostered understanding on all sides. She thought about Brol - who was sitting behind her in the far back of the room - and wished she could tell him a truth or two about how it felt to be used as his personal punching bag.

Scholar Monk interrupted her thoughts by swooping down the aisle to check everyone's work. She shoved the book underneath her tunic and bent quickly over her blank parchment

Too late. Scholar Monk swept it up. Ari Ara sighed and resigned herself to weathering his tirade. She could hardly tell the difference between Old Tongue and modern Marianan, let alone write an essay on how to translate one into the other. She stared at the floor, waiting for him to finish, wondering what her punishment was going to be.

"Why do we only study war?" Minli's voice interrupted.

"What?" Scholar Monk spluttered, surprised by the interruption and the nature of the question.

"Why do we only study war?" Minli repeated, his eyes wide with innocence. "Battles, causes of conflict, strategy, commanders, rulers . . . why don't we ever study, oh I don't know, poetry?"

"You study the epic poems - "

"They're all about war," Minli pointed out.

"But this is Monk's Hand Monastery," Scholar Monk explained, blinking owlishly. "We train warriors."

"But what if one doesn't want to be a warrior?" Minli asked quietly.

"Or can't be a warrior, you mean," Brol mocked from the back of the room.

Minli flushed.

"I've got two legs," Ari Ara said heatedly, rising to Minli's defense, "and I don't want to be a warrior."

"Those who want to learn another trade go to apprenticeships or to the Sisters in Mari Valley. They are funded to train girls - "

" - and cripples," Brol muttered.

" - in the arts of *Anar*, the Gentle Way. We are funded to train warriors."

"So, you're soldiers, then," Ari Ara commented with a hint of scorn in her voice.

"Mind your tongue!" Scholar Monk scolded.

"But, it's true," Minli cried, his eyes wide with new understanding. "You teach war because you're paid to teach it. War buys your bread."

"And yours, orphan," Scholar Monk reminded him sternly.

"I wouldn't be an orphan if not for war!" Minli shot back. "I didn't ask to live here. I didn't ask to lose my leg!"

He looked close to tears.

"Like it or leave it," Brol snarled from the back of the room. "Go study *Anar* with the girls."

Scholar Monk unexpectedly turned on the older boy.

"That's enough, Brol," he snapped. "There are many of us here at Monk's Hand who do not train in *Attar*, but who serve in other ways. The senior monks, the archivist, myself. Many of us were orphans, too, you know."

"You were?" Ari Ara blurted out in surprise.

"Yes, of course," Scholar Monk replied, equally taken aback. "Surely you knew that?"

Heads shook around the room.

"Many of the older monks are orphans from the earlier wars," Scholar Monk said softly. "Or from Border Mountain skirmishes or the sicknesses that swept the region. Some of us lost homes or farms and turned to the spiritual path because there was nothing left for us. Or we came to the lectures held by the monks, hungry for the bread and soup served afterward. My family fled our home and came to the Capital; my sisters and mother to serve the wealthy, and my brothers to enlist in the military, seeking to avenge my father's death. I was too young, but of course wanted to fight. However, I'm afraid I showed far more aptitude for pounding history into dense heads than for pounding dense heads into history."

Scholar Monk cast a sorrowful smile around the room at his little play on words. From the stunned expressions on the young children's faces, he judged that his story had reached them.

"Let's pray that the Lost Heir is found before war breaks out again," he murmured.

"So it's true?" Ari Ara blurted out.

"I hope not," Scholar Monk said with a shudder, "but I'd advise you all to study hard . . . and train even harder."

He scowled at Ari Ara for a moment.

"Now, back to your work, everyone."

He swept back up to the front of the class. Ari Ara's eyes widened as she realized he had forgotten to punish her. She glanced at Minli. He smirked.

Third Brother, he mouthed.

Ari Ara smothered her laugh. Minli's distraction had, indeed, been a trick straight out of Alaren's book.

During the latter part of class, Scholar Monk launched into such a fast-paced lecture on the wars of his lifetime that no one had time for daydreaming or questions; they were too busy taking notes. At the end of class, Ari Ara sighed with relief and started clearing away her parchment.

"We've got to find the Lost Heir," Minli murmured. "There's been messenger hawks coming and going all week from the Capital, and each time one arrives Head Monk comes out of his office looking more worried than before."

Ari Ara nodded in agreement. She thought of Fanten Grandmother and her secrets, but the old woman would be deep underground until spring, buried in trance-sleep. Ari Ara leaned on her hand on top of Third Brother's book and bent over the aisle to whisper to Minli.

"Let's go over the clues in the prophecy again tonight."

Minli nodded. Ari Ara straightened and reached to pick up her brushes.

"What's that on your palm?" Minli said, turning her hand over to see.

A patterned circle was imprinted on her skin.

With a cry, he pointed to the cover of the Third Brother's book.

"Look!"

"What?" she asked, confused.

"Remember the prophecy? *By the Mark of Peace, the lost one is found.*"

He placed his hand on the symbol imprinted into the leather cover and pressed down. Minli counted to ten. He raised his hand. A circle with a set of rippling patterns marked his skin.

Ari Ara gasped.

"The Mark of the Lost Heir?!"

"Maybe," Minli qualified, though his brown eyes gleamed with excitement. "I'm not sure. This was the symbol of the old country before Marin and Shirar split the world."

Ari Ara furrowed her brow, trying to remember the lesson. Minli launched into an explanation.

"Marin and Shirar split the world into two nations using the Border Mountains as the dividing line. Everything to the east became Mariana, with the Capital situated on an island in the middle of Mari River. Everything to the west, Shirar took as his desert kingdom."

"Oh, right," Ari Ara added, remembering a story in the Third Brother's book, "and Alaren bitterly protested the whole affair, suspecting that it would lead to war. He took the old symbol of unity as his emblem and swore to work for peace and reconciliation. That's why the symbol's on his book," she concluded, pleased with herself.

Minli turned the book one way and pointed at one part of the circle.

"Water."

He turned the book the other way.

"Desert."

"A perfect mark to identify an heir to both thrones," she agreed, staring at her palm. "It's fading now, but on the Lost Heir it must be something permanent like a tattoo or a brand."

Minli frowned in thought.

"Oh!" he exclaimed, grabbing his crutch. "That's it!"

"That's what?" she called as he rushed out the door.

He didn't answer and she was left scratching her head at his behavior.

That evening, Minli hobbled over with an enormous book tucked under his arm. He tilted his head toward the copy room. Ari Ara abandoned her spot by the warm fire in the Main Hall, ran to fetch her shepherdess cloak, and met Minli in the cool dark room.

"What have you got there?" she asked Minli.

"Records," the boy answered, dropping the heavy volume on the table with a thud. "Birth records for every child in Mariana, orphan or otherwise, born roughly nine to twelve years ago. Name, parentage, gender . . . and any notable features, deformities, birthmarks, or scars."

"The monks keep track of all that?" she asked in amazement.

Minli gave her a wry look.

"Would you like to know what Marin and Shirar ate for breakfast before they split the world?" he asked, only half-joking. "Come on, let's get started. The Lost Heir is bound to be in here somewhere."

Line by line, they studied the fine print. By the time they heard voices leaving the Main Hall for sleeping quarters, their eyes were burning, their feet were half-frozen, and they had gone through nearly half the record book. They had three potential candidates . . . none of which seemed very likely. Although each was recorded as having a mark, one was almost too old, another was described as having a ghastly scar spread over half her face, and the third had died of fever at the age of six.

"The problem," Minli mused, "is that people rarely stay where they started. We have birth records, but we don't know where most of them are located now."

"Or even that the heir's still alive," she pointed out.

"Or in Mariana. The heir could be in the desert, you know."

"We'll never narrow it down," Ari Ara moaned.

"Yes, we will," Minli said with a gleam in his eye, "starting with these records. We have to think practically, eliminate the possibilities one-by-one, and then look at what remains."

"You sound like Shulen," she grumbled, thinking of her first lesson in *Azar*.

"Well, we have to keep searching," he urged.

"Yes," Ari Ara groaned. "Line by line."

They bent their heads back over the record book.

"What are you two doing?"

They spun at the sound. Ari Ara wiped the guilty expression off her face and elbowed Minli to do the same. Scholar Monk stood in the doorway, frowning at them.

"We're researching," Minli answered.

"For what?"

"Minli's looking for his family," Ari Ara blurted out.

Scholar Monk's expression softened.

"My dear children, we don't know where Minli came from. We are glad that he is here, however."

"We were just hoping to find some clues," Minli said.

Scholar Monk smiled gently.

"Very well, but don't stay up all night."

Then he left, shutting the door against the drafts.

They sighed with relief and turned back to the table.

"What if the Lost Heir isn't an orphan?" Ari Ara asked, rubbing her eyes. "What if he's being raised as somebody's son? You know, hidden."

"We'd still have a record of birth and unusual markings," Minli insisted, "and remember, the Lost Heir could be a girl."

"But he or she could be recorded incorrectly . . . for secrecy."

Minli looked aghast.

"A monk would never intentionally record facts inaccurately!" he gasped.

Ari Ara rolled her eyes. Minli started to lecture her about the ethics of scribes and monks.

"What if they make an honest mistake?" she said, mostly to shut him up. She thought her first suggestion was more likely - anyone could be bribed.

"Monks make very few mistakes," Minli informed her huffily.

"My record's not in there," she argued, pointing to the volume.

"Of course not," Minli countered. "They don't record Fanten births."

"I'm not Fanten," she reminded him. "And what if you just don't have a record on the Lost Heir?"

Minli shook his head, appalled at the idea. Ari Ara flipped through the pages, scowling at a sudden thought.

"Why isn't your record in here?"

"It is, but as a footnote, see?" Minli stopped her hand and opened to a page in the back of the record book. "Somewhere, I'm recorded at birth, under whatever name my unknown parents gave me. However, since I'm a foundling, I have a separate record under *Minli*, which is the name the monks gave me."

He pointed. Next to the year and date was the short note:

Minli, left at Monk's Hand Monastery by unknown person(s), parentage unknown, missing right leg.

"You could be the Lost Heir," Ari Ara mused.

"No mark," he pointed out swiftly. He shot her a rueful look. "Don't think I haven't considered it."

"But what if the Mark isn't on the heir's body. What if it's on a secret record that says - "

"Minli, the one-legged orphan, is the Lost Heir?" he mocked, raising an eyebrow.

"It's just a suggestion," she grumbled.

"Not a very likely one," he snorted. "Got any other bright ideas?"

"No," she sighed.

As they bent back over the record book, Ari Ara shook her head. He was such an old monk.

CHAPTER FOURTEEN

· · · · ·

Between reading and record searching, as her ribs healed and stopped aching, Ari Ara began to share outer *Azar* with Minli. In the dark storeroom, deep in the side of the mountain where neither the howl of the winter blizzards nor the noise of the monastery could be heard, they spent their evening hours exploring the Way Between.

From the beginning, they framed their sessions as experiments. Ari Ara was just an apprentice. Minli harbored doubts about his ability. Neither knew if it was possible for a one-legged boy to learn *Azar*.

"But the Way Between is all about unknown possibilities," Ari Ara stated, trying to ease the nervousness in her friend's face, "so we might as well find out."

She tied up her leg with a piece of cloth, wrapping her calf to her thigh so she had to learn to think and move like her friend. At first, she grinned confidently, standing poised on one foot. She launched into the lecture Shulen had given on the first day, moved to demonstrate her point, stepped onto a foot that wasn't there, and landed in a heap below him.

She rolled over. Minli's brown eyes creased with laughter as he looked down at her. Ari Ara pushed back up to standing, hopping as she found her balance.

"Alright," she conceded, "let's just figure it out as we go."

Balance, stillness, subtlety, strength . . . one by one, they concocted ways to develop and explore each dimension of *Azar.* The one-legged world, Ari Ara soon discovered, differed vastly from her habitual movement patterns. It was Minli who adapted the seven ways to roll and challenged her to learn the new forms. She showed him the ten ways to spring and he promptly invented an eleventh. By the end of the first week, his nervousness gave way to enthusiasm as he found his friend had a sense of humor and unexpected depths of patience.

For all of her temper and impetuousness, Ari Ara was also perceptive. She had caught a glimpse of the inner turmoil of her friend on the first day. He held a deep fear of failing at physical tasks, ingrained by a lifetime of callous remarks and casual dismissals. In a monastery devoted to the skills of warriors, he was ignored and shunted to the side. He excelled at studies and scribing, that was true, but he also burned with a feverish need to prove his merit and worth to the rest of the monastery. There were many who questioned his presence and had suggested sending him away. The old archivist and Scholar Monk argued for the boy, however, and he tried to make himself useful in their eyes.

But now, in the gloom of the storeroom, every new motion kicked back at years of insults and slights; every accomplishment in *Azar* struck down hundreds of memories of being marginalized and shunned. When Ari Ara stumbled over her "missing" leg and picked herself up from the floor with a groan, he saw himself learning to navigate a world built for two legs, adapting every action to his one-legged perspective.

144

He was learning more from *Azar* practices than simply how to balance, fall, dodge, roll, spring, and rise . . . and the new range of physical motion exhilarated him. His muscles ached at night in a blend of contentment and complaint. The practices challenged him in ways he'd never expected as he learned to move in ways he had never imagined!

They hit hard spots and stumbling blocks. There were times when Minli's frustration boiled over and burst out in hot tears. Ari Ara would crouch down beside him at a loss for words as she heard him echo the lies he'd been told over the years.

"I can't," he would spit out bitterly. "I'll never learn. I just can't do it. I'm pathetic. You shouldn't even bother with me."

"Yes, I should," she'd argue. "You're teaching me how to read and write . . . and you're doing a lot better at this than I am at those brushstrokes."

Minli smiled weakly. She had a point. Ari Ara had a genius for movement, but the written realm drove her mad, shape shifting under her eyes, wiggling into incorrect meanings. While she'd made headway on reading characters, her written characters and brushstrokes remained largely illegible.

"Come on," she bargained. "One more try at this exercise, and then I promise to practice those characters you tried to teach me this morning."

By midwinter, Ari Ara couldn't catch him every time they practiced *Azar*'s training of tagging and dodging. And, if she held back from the full range of her speed, he sometimes managed to surprise her in a blind spot or miscalculation. His gleeful satisfaction at those successes gave him confidence and Ari Ara quietly realized how Shulen did the same for her. She started to tease the edges of his capacity, using her awareness to help expand the front line of his growth.

One evening, Ari Ara eyed Minli's crutch.

"We should practice with that, too," she said.

She fashioned a crutch out of an old mop and they explored the new motions the wooden sticks opened up to the practice. They learned to balance against the solidity of the pole, spring and launch off its point, dodge the sweep of its range, and nudge each other off-balance with just enough force to move the body, but without leaving a bruise on the skin.

They practiced how to regain the crutch if it was lost and how to use it to block an attack. Ari Ara managed to lever her whole body up and over the mop handle so high that she nearly hit the ceiling of the storeroom. They gained bruises in mishaps, but discovered a whole new field of motion. Minli practiced balancing on his foot while she ducked his swipes with the crutch. He drilled her on one leg then made her untie the first and switch to the other. Then he made her practice with both legs. She gained levels of speed and agility that awed him and gave him a sense of pride at being able to contribute to her training. Even Shulen noticed the difference when their morning practices resumed.

"A bit of rest did you good," he commented.

Ari Ara told Minli about it later and he grinned.

Minli advanced diligently. He had none of Ari Ara's stubbornness, but far more persistence. Where *Azar* came to her as naturally as breathing, he worked through the physical challenges piece-by-piece, resolutely studying the form until he mastered it. Ari Ara took note of his approach and applied it to brushstrokes. Secretly, it rankled her that his *Azar* was progressing more rapidly than her writing!

Minli might never be as fast or strong as Emir Miresh, she reflected one day, but he could hold his own against any village boy. And, when it came to inner *Azar*, he already ran circles around her understanding. He was as clever as Alaren, himself!

Her temper still moved faster than her wits, but Minli had an ingenious reply to everything. By midwinter, he had read the Third Brother's book backwards and forwards, and even began inventing scenarios of his own. If they held a Trial in *Azar*, she was convinced he would come away the Champion. She'd win some matches and lose others, but he'd talk his challengers into surrendering before the official Trial even began!

The day she finally read the last page of the book was a moment of triumph for both of them. They sat for a long time in comfortable silence in the storeroom, throats too tight for words until the afternoon bell rang out and they had to run to avoid being late for chores. Just before the outside entryway to the courtyard, Ari Ara tugged Minli's sleeve.

"Thank you," she murmured.

She squeezed him tightly, so he could not see the moisture shining in her eyes. She, an orphan who belonged to no one, could now read and write like the monks, the nobles, and even the Great Ones!

Minli said nothing, but returned the embrace. There were no words that the one-legged boy could say to the girl who had replaced his fear with graceful strength.

Shulen caught a glimpse of them as they parted. A bemused smile flitted across his craggy face. *It worked*, he thought, watching the pair enter the kitchen. The lame boy could hold his own . . . and the wild shepherdess could finally read.

CHAPTER FIFTEEN

. . . . .

Ari Ara thought her life might be absolutely perfect if not for Brol. After Head Monk ordered him out of training sessions, Ari Ara felt his resentment stabbing her like a knife in her back. He seethed in the corner of her vision. She avoided him as much as possible, sitting on opposite ends of any room they both occupied and never speaking to him.

The winter turned a corner out of solid ice. The breeze began to tease back and forth with scents of thawing snow. After the long months staying cooped up indoors, old frictions rubbed raw. Even Nobstick and Teapot Monk grew huffy and short-tempered with one another. Ari Ara avoided everyone but Shulen and threw herself into her studies and trainings with fervor. When Nobstick assigned her to go fetch eggs from the village, she leapt at the chance to get out of the cloistered walls of the winter-bound monastery.

The sun melted the snow off the long steps. Icicles dripped from the tall statues and ancestor pillars that lined the landings. Ari Ara could see the heavy dampness of the white peaks of the mountainsides. *It won't be long now*, she thought. In a few more

149

weeks, the river would thunder with snowmelt. She breathed in the sharp, humid air and smiled.

Collecting the basket-carriers of eggs was uneventful, but time consuming. The village head had messages to relay to the monks and the old aunties wanted to hear all the gossip. Everyone asked after Shulen, and how the trainings were proceeding, and if the monks had heard from the Capital. Finally, Ari Ara managed to break away. She shouldered the padded wooden stick that bore the heavy load of the two laden baskets of eggs. Climbing the stairs was hard work, but she was pleased to find that she took them easily, hardly winded at all.

Halfway up, Brol was waiting for her. She stepped warily onto the middle landing, trying to calculate how she would get past him. Burdened with the eggs, there was no way she could outrun him.

"Let me pass, Brol," she said as he barred her path.

His only response was to flip her hair into her eyes. With her arms holding the padded yoke, she could only blow it away with a breath of exasperation.

Don't be provoked, she told herself silently.

"Well, well," he drawled. "We meet again."

She said nothing and attempted to step around him. He blocked her path again. Ari Ara's blue-grey eyes met his coldly.

"Don't pick a fight, Brol."

"Me?" he held his arms up in a mock gesture of innocence. "I would never presume to antagonize Shulen's pet. Oh no. Not when the old warrior has a grudge against me already."

Ari Ara thought of a dozen quick retorts and decided against them all.

"He'll regret pampering you when your desert blood goes berserk," he snarled. "They all go crazy, you know, the desert demons. Butcher everything in sight - men, women, children, even dogs."

Ari Ara clenched her teeth over the rising fire in her hot blood. *Master it,* she ordered herself sharply, *like Shulen said.*

"You should have been left to the wolves," Brol taunted.

"They tried, Brol," she retorted, "but the wolves wouldn't eat me. I'm too tough."

She bared her lips in a snarl of smile.

"Let me pass."

"No."

He shoved one of her shoulders, then the other. The egg baskets swung precariously back and forth. She teetered on the edge of the landing.

"Come on, Brol, stop it. There's a week's worth of eggs in here."

"How many chores of punishment will you get if you drop it?"

He knocked her arms off the wooden yoke and the baskets rocked wildly. She twisted to see his next move, but he was too fast. His blow caught her in an awkward position. She tumbled down the steps. Hundreds of eggs shattered and rolled in all directions. The sound of his laughter chased her.

"What happened?" Shulen barked when she finally dragged herself into the courtyard, covered in shells and egg yolks, empty baskets in hand.

"I fell," she muttered. "Got distracted on my way back."

Brol smirked in the shadows of an overhang.

"With a week's worth of eggs?" Shulen scolded with a frown.

Ari Ara hung her head.

"Yes," she answered in a low voice.

"Go apologize to the kitchen monks. You're assigned to them for the next week instead of trainings."

"But - " she started to object.

"And you'll wash the steps now, sweep off the shells, scrub the yolk clean, then get yourself cleaned up."

"But - "

"No arguments. You need to learn to be more careful."

Shulen turned back to the trainees and snapped at them to stop gawking and get back to practice. Covered in eggshells, slimy yolk, and bruises, Ari Ara glared at them all. She tromped to the kitchen, endured the inevitable berating, and then collected a pair of buckets.

"Use the lower well," Shulen commanded as she went to draw water.

"In the village?" she complained.

"Go."

She kicked the ground furiously and stormed out of the courtyard. Why did he have to make everything so hard? It would be twice as difficult to lug the water up, as it would be to carry it down. And now, not only would the entire monastery be laughing at her, but the villagers would be, too.

At the gateway, Minli stood leaning on his crutch, holding out a small sack.

"Dinner," he said.

"I'm not hungry," she snapped back.

"You will be later, and I'm not climbing down the stairs in the dark," he argued persuasively. "You should have just told Shulen that Brol pushed you."

"How do you know that?"

"Heard him chortling over it when he got back."

"He's horrid."

"Yeah," Minli agreed, handing the sack to her. "That's why I stuck a couple of rotten eggs under his bed. He'll never notice until it's too late."

A smile teased her lips.

"Thanks, Minli."

"It's nothing," he shrugged. "I'm already spreading rumors that *somebody* farts in his sleep."

Ari Ara burst out laughing and took off down the steps feeling better than she had coming up.

A silent war broke out. Ari Ara acquired a new bruise each day. Brol was fast, malicious, and a fiend for catching her in the ribs when no one was looking. Ari Ara cynically suspected that he was another awful training concocted by Shulen to test her patience.

"If he is," she muttered, "I'm not failing this test. Brol can't provoke me . . . and he won't always get away with this." She vowed she'd find a way to stop him.

Brol split a sack of flour on her one day in the storeroom, then howled with laughter as she spluttered and sneezed. Ari Ara glared at him, then stomped off to get the broom. She stalked into the Main Hall for evening chants stark white as a ghost and when Shulen told her to go clean up, she retorted,

"I wore the eggs. I'll wear the flour. Pretty soon you can throw me into the fire and bake a cake."

The senior monks chuckled at the joke, but she had to sweep half the monastery for her impertinence. Shulen, however, started keeping a closer eye on his apprentice. The next time Brol blamed her for breaking a stack of plates, Shulen barked at him to get a broom and clean it up. Brol stared at Shulen in disbelief until the older man grabbed Ari Ara by the scruff of her shirt and hauled her after him. Brol smirked, certain that Shulen was about to whip her.

Instead, he tossed Ari Ara into his quarters, slid the door shut, and said in a frustrated tone,

"Either deal with him soon or this monastery will break into pieces."

"What?!" she exclaimed in surprise.

"Do you think I'm blind?" he shot back. "I find it hard to believe that a girl who can stand all day atop an ancestor pillar would lose her balance on a broad landing while carrying eggs. It's difficult to imagine you being clumsy enough to break a sack of flour and a stack of dishes, knock over a shelf of scrolls, trip over a dirty wash bucket in the Main Hall, forget the senior monks' robes in the snow, and rip a hole in the Head Monk's ceremonial robe all in one month. I don't believe it."

Ari Ara stared at him open-mouthed. Shulen sat down on his mat and studied her with a combination of humor and concern.

"I know those bruises didn't come from practicing *Azar*," he commented, indicating the latest, "because you haven't had a spare moment for training due to all the extra punishments you've been given."

Ari Ara bit her bottom lip.

"But what am I supposed to do about him?" she complained, plopping down across from Shulen.

"Tell the Head Monk," Shulen suggested, watching her carefully.

"That's *Anar's* way," Ari Ara replied. "I can't always expect someone bigger or more powerful to protect me."

"You want to challenge him to a match of *Attar* in the courtyard?" Shulen guessed with a wry laugh.

"He'd cream me," Ari Ara muttered.

"Probably not as quick as you think," Shulen commented, "but he is twice your height and weight, quick and well trained. One good solid kick would send you halfway across the courtyard."

Ari Ara sighed and picked a loose straw in the mat.

"There's always a Way Between," Shulen encouraged her. "Think about it until you see it clearly."

CHAPTER SIXTEEN

. . . . .

Temperamental, the weather turned a cold shoulder on Monk's Hand. A wet, sticky sleet plastered the forests, slopes, and the monastery. The trainings which had been enthusiastically moved into the muddy training grounds returned to the Main Hall for a few days with the tables and benches shoved up against the walls. Ari Ara stationed herself near the door so she could observe the sparring matches. She followed all the trainings avidly, but with increasing confusion.

"Why do they take hits they could have avoided?" she asked Shulen later.

Shulen had increased her *Azar* practices to twice daily. In addition, he gave her assignments to practice on her own. Her body ached and protested, but working with Minli in secret helped her rise to Shulen's challenges.

"Sometimes, they don't see the blows coming," Shulen said, answering her question. "They're not quite as quick as you are, you know."

She didn't know. She wasn't allowed to spar with the other trainees. Ari Ara worked only with Shulen . . . and he seemed as far beyond her as ever.

"And," Shulen continued thoughtfully, absently whirling aside as she tried to tag him in their practice, "sometimes they want to be hit."

"Why would anyone want that?" she scoffed, ducking under his swinging leg.

"To toughen themselves up and then prove how tough they are," he explained.

She frowned and narrowly avoided his attempt to tag her.

"But why?" she asked again. "What's the point of being tough?"

Shulen laughed.

"Good question, kitten. Let me know when you find the answer."

It did not occur to her that Shulen was speaking rhetorically. She assumed that he was giving her another assignment. She pondered it as she studied the trainees and monks, searching for the answer.

"They're afraid," she decided. "Afraid that if they don't act tough, they'll get hurt by someone bigger and stronger than them."

She thought about Shulen, undeniably the fastest, strongest, and toughest of them all. No one dared to challenge Shulen. She glanced at Teapot Monk, fat and red-faced. No one challenged him, either.

"Better to be a cook than a warrior," Ari Ara muttered to herself. "When Shulen gets old, somebody's going to beat him, but nobody bothers the cook. We all like our bread and soup too much."

Ari Ara paused in the doorway of the kitchen as a flash of insight struck her. An image of Teapot Monk in the whirling steam of the pots and pans. A memory of Shulen dancing in the snow more gentle than anyone in the world would imagine. A vision of how to deal with Brol.

The fickle spring blew back to warm. The courtyard melted into puddles and mud, then dried out. Shulen moved the trainings outdoors. Ari Ara tracked Brol throughout the days, waiting for her chance. One morning, when Scholar Monk assigned him extra copying work, she made her move.

"Want a sweet roll?" she offered, carrying a plate toward Brol as he worked on a scroll in the empty copy room.

"What?"

"Sweet roll," she repeated. "Just out of the oven. I thought you might want one."

"Is this a joke?" he asked, glaring at her with his dark eyebrows meeting in the middle.

"If I was going to poison you, I would have done it ages ago," she pointed out, truthfully.

Brol sneered. She shrugged.

"What do you want?" he demanded.

To dance with the snow, she thought silently. Out loud she said,

"Why do you hate me? What did I ever do to you?"

"You exist, demon," Brol growled. "That alone is enough."

He flung down his brush and crossed his arms over his chest, glowering at her.

"I was first in the Trials this fall," he spat out. "I worked hard for that honor. With Shulen here," he swallowed the bitterness of unrealized hopes, "that apprenticeship should have gone to me, not some desert demon whose hair is as red as - "

He stopped.

"Get out of here," he snarled, bending back over the scroll and hiding his expression.

Ari Ara took a breath. It was now or never.

"As red as what?"

Brol stilled. He did not look up as he spoke.

"The man who killed my family had hair like yours."

Her stomach clenched. She exhaled. *Alaren help me,* she prayed silently as she set the sweet roll plate down on the table and tensed to spring away if he lashed out at her.

"What happened?" she asked. Her stomach dropped a nervous mile.

"None of your business," Brol shot back curtly, looking up with venom in his eyes.

"Did you fight him off?" she guessed.

"I'd have killed him if I could," Brol said in a voice so cold it froze the blood in her veins.

"You - you must have been really young," she commented.

"Six." Brol spat out in self-disgust. "Old enough to remember, too young to do anything."

"I know the feeling," Ari Ara muttered thoughtlessly, thinking about the time he beat her up in the village.

"No, you don't!" Brol screamed furiously at her, leaping up on the bench and leaning dangerously across the table at her, eyes half-crazed with memories. "You don't remember your mother's throat bleeding or your siblings sliced open around you or your father crumbling over a sword. You don't know what it's like to do nothing as they hurt you and laugh at the same time."

"Oh no?" she snapped back, shoving the sweet roll plate across the table angrily. "Haven't you been doing that to me all year? Punching me? Laughing at me?!"

They were both yelling now.

"You think that's going to bring them back?!" she hollered.

"Shut up!" he ordered, pounding the table with his fist.

"You're just like them!" Ari Ara accused him angrily. "Proving you're tough by hurting everyone, especially anyone too small to fight back."

He lunged across the table.

"Oh no, you don't!" she retorted, dodging away. "I'm sorry I remind you of what happened to your family - "

She broke off to dart across the copy room as he chased her. She spun out of reach, surprised to find that she meant it; she was sorry to remind him of his worst horrors.

"If hurting me could bring them back, I might let you do it," she told him, leaping up and over the table. "But it won't."

He howled at her and thrust a kick at her head that could have split a solid stone. She ducked it.

"It won't stop you from hurting either!" she warned him.

His muscles bunched to spring and Ari Ara saw it a mile away. It was like the snow . . . there was a wind of hurt that moved him. She could see it, even if he couldn't.

"You won't ever lay a hand on me again, Brol," she promised ferociously. "So, you'd best deal with your anger some other way."

He moved like lightning, but she darted with the speed of the Way Between, through the copy room, out the door into the Teaching Room; over, around, and through the desks, ignoring the startled orphans and Scholar Monk's shocked chastisements. He nearly caught her in the Main Hall, but she ducked into the chaos of the kitchen and he dropped behind. She burst out of the other door into the courtyard and stood in the center of the open space despite the surprised protests of the trainees. The senior monks under the eaves jolted out of their midday meditations.

161

She turned and waited. Brol skidded to a halt on the edge of the courtyard. The eyes of the trainees and monks pinned him in place. His face turned red.

"What's going on?" Shulen demanded.

Ari Ara tossed her hair out of her eyes and replied in a tone that made Shulen look sharply at her.

"We're finishing this." She stared at the glowering youth across the courtyard, daring him to challenge her out in the open, in front of everyone. "Right, Brol?"

Brol's eyes narrowed into furious slits. She waited. His breath hissed between his clenched teeth. His fury boiled under his skin. His muscles tensed.

The moment opened like a door. Ari Ara saw his leap coming in slow motion. She stepped through the possibilities between fighting or fleeing, and entered the Way Between. As Brol sprung at her, Ari Ara turned his momentum in midair. Softly as a snowflake in Shulen's hand, she leveraged his flying weight into a flip and brought his body to the ground.

"It ends here, Brol," she warned him in a low voice as his shocked eyes stared up at her. She held his gaze for a moment until she saw something shift in his face. Then she stepped back and strode out of the monastery without another word.

CHAPTER SEVENTEEN

. . . . .

The next morning, Shulen slid back the door of her closet.

"Up," he said in a low tone that brooked no arguments.

Ari Ara gulped, certain she was in trouble for yesterday's showdown with Brol. She rolled out and followed him to the dark and hushed courtyard.

"Show me what you did to Brol," Shulen demanded.

"Uh . . . I'm not sure," she stammered, scratching her head to wake up. "I just . . . " She made the motion of bringing a snowflake to the ground.

"Interesting," Shulen commented. "Who taught you that?"

"You did," she replied, feeling dull-witted.

"Me?" Shulen answered, astonished.

"Yes, in the snow. Remember?" Ari Ara made the movement again, tracing a descending spiral. He imitated it.

"Hmm. Try it on me."

And he leapt as Brol had.

Ari Ara hardly had time to react. She slid sideways, pushed slightly against the lever of his motion, and tipped him toward the ground.

"Again," Shulen commanded.

Several repetitions later, he barked, "Now you! Leap!"

Ari Ara obeyed. Shulen caught her momentum and rolled her to the ground.

"Again."

Ari Ara sprang from a crouch, but this time, as Shulen practiced the move, she intentionally nudged him off-balance. They tumbled and he threw her a surprised glance.

"Good, very good. Now, try this," he ordered. "Try to unbalance me with *Azar*. Use my momentum to take me off my feet. Turn every attack into a fall. Go!"

He launched into motion.

Ari Ara dodged out of the way.

"Try it!" he barked.

Fed up with his commands so early in the morning, she planted her feet, grabbed his arm, and let his force carry his torso slightly past hers. Then she leaned into his weight and levered him into a fall. He rolled over his shoulder and returned to standing, wheeling for another attack. She darted aside twice before her chance came. Shift, lever, drop. He flipped and rolled.

When Shulen rose, intensity crackled from his every gesture. He flexed into position and leapt into *Attar*. Instinctively, she threw up her hands to block his strike, felt the first weight of connecting pressure, pushed back just enough to make him engage his muscles . . . then she released, dropping her hands, leaping backwards into the fall of gravity, and letting him stumble in surprise. He lunged, twisted, and spun out a kick that would have broken her newly healed ribs, except that she leapt aside - and clamped his foot under her arm as she did. Riding his momentum in freefall, her extra weight pulled him off-balance again. It was like Brol and the wooden crutch, she recalled as she awkwardly landed on the floor.

164

"Ooph," she groaned.

Shulen stood up and shook out his leg as he offered her a hand up.

"Interesting."

"You keep saying that," she remarked in a sour tone.

"What are the principles?" he asked, ignoring her complaint.

It was part of her trainings; each time she learned a new technique, he grilled her on the principles underlying the lesson. Ari Ara rubbed her shoulder while she mulled the answer.

"Momentum. I'm using your forward force to bring you off balance."

"Good. What else?"

"Let you exert . . . don't push. I'm using *Azar* to get out of the way until, again, you fall out of balance."

"Yes."

"And stay out of the places you expect me to be."

Shulen chuckled.

"Given your record at chores and lessons, you're quite skilled at that."

Ari Ara rolled her eyes.

"I also used your own limbs as levers against you . . . like that time with your arm." She demonstrated the gesture that had flipped him onto his back.

"Yes, well done. And you?" he asked. "What were you doing?"

"Falling all over the place," she grumbled.

Shulen lifted an eyebrow.

"I was spiraling," she sighed, answering the question more precisely. "I was using descending circles like the snowflake, letting gravity take care of things."

"Yes, remember that. Gravity is the friend of small people. Like the birds, gravity does not hold you as tightly as us heavyweights. If you work with gravity, she'll pull your opponent back down to Earth for you. She's much stronger than you are; even the largest mountains stand no chance of breaking free of her grip."

Shulen set them back to practice, working through move after move, repeating, studying, testing. He explained each move with infinite detail, drilling them both in using *Azar* to disarm the attacks of *Attar*.

When the morning bell rang, Shulen told her to practice on her own.

"Study the warriors-in-training, too. Look for the Way Between the techniques that they're learning, but don't tell anyone what you're doing. I want to surprise everyone someday when *Azar* demonstrates that it can always topple *Attar*."

Some subtle energy shifted between them. As winter surrendered to spring, Ari Ara noticed that the dynamic of her trainings with Shulen had shifted from an apprentice learning from her master to a pair of fellow explorers investigating new levels of *Azar*. Shulen stopped drilling her and instead opened a space of inquiry and study.

"That!" Shulen exclaimed, watching her one morning. "What was that?"

Ari Ara froze. She retraced her steps, swaying like the fickle spring wind that teased them, blowing hot then cold, here then gone. Shulen whirled into the dance and she nearly laughed at his attempts to guess her unexpected moves.

She learned to never be where expected, and to always be where he didn't suspect. She levered his heavier weight against the carefully placed pivot points of her stances, pouring his momentum and mass into the ground rather than into her smaller muscles. She aligned her bones with the Earth and spun like the wind. In *Azar,* she poured like water, finding the subtle routes, the cracks in the stones, the slivers of openings in tight spaces. Together, she and Shulen were finding a new Way Between . . . an expression of *Azar* that not only confronted force without striking back, but also transformed the attack, changed it, redirected its energy, and moved the other person into a place where they could not cause harm.

"We could do anything with this!" Ari Ara enthused. "Even the Lost Heir's Champion could be a follower of *Azar!*"

Shulen chuckled at her wild imaginings, but his eyes looked thoughtful, very thoughtful. As her skill grew, Shulen watched her with an added layer of scrutiny. *Azar* came to the girl as naturally as breathing. He sensed it tingling through her veins along with her blood. Shulen spent many sleepless nights wondering. At times, it seemed as if *Azar* was a force that had simply lain dormant in her marrow, needing only the slightest encouragement to come singing out through her bones. Shulen knew of only one bloodline for whom that was possible . . . and he had long believed the last child of that lineage was gone forever, buried too young in a very small grave, a victim of violence like so many others.

And then he buried his wild hopes in cynicism, telling himself that he was simply imagining what he wanted to see in a curve of a smile, a gesture, a tone of laughter. He looked to the Fanten Forest, still shrouded in shadows, and began counting the days until the Fanten Grandmother would awaken. As the redheaded girl whipped through the Way Between, Shulen strengthened his resolve to confront the elusive old woman. They had bones to pick between them.

CHAPTER EIGHTEEN

. . . . .

Up. Down. Back. Around. The scent of change rode the crosswinds. As the crackle of spring charged her with bursting energy, Shulen sent Ari Ara running the steps of Monk's Hand from monastery to village to the Thumb's Pass and back again. Each day at dawn, their feet seemed to touch the floor at the same instant, and stretch into stride together.

"Azar!" he cried from landings as he waited for her to return.

"Azar!" she called up to the echoing steep slopes of the mountains.

"Azar!" he challenged in the sandy courtyard of the monastery. They spun and wheeled under, over, around, and between.

She gained speed and stamina. Those afternoon trainings must be wearing Shulen down, Ari Ara grumbled to herself, seeing sweat break out on his brow one morning in practice. Then the grey-haired Stone One whirled and she barely ducked in time.

The day came when the breathless pulse of spring cracked open the snowcaps on the High Mountains and sent a flashflood raging through the Monk's Tears River. The roar of

169

the water echoed through the entire valley. A wild excitement flooded the air. The budding trees trembled in exuberance. Water tumbled down every rock and stream. The stones sang in tongues of melting snow. Ari Ara trilled the Fanten cry, sharp and distinctive. She shaded her eyes and looked to the forest. In the caves below the Great Trees, the Fanten would be stirring as restlessly as the water above them. The whole world was awakening in the flush of spring, stretching its limbs and dancing in delight. The monks prepared for the annual spring ceremony. The courtyard teemed with a flurry of grey robes as they rolled out the Great Gongs and readied the Horns.

"Here it comes," Minli warned.

She was about to ask what he meant when the Horns erupted. The strength of the bellow made her step back a pace. Loose pebbles rattled on the stone steps. In the courtyard, the sonorous crescendo of the Great Gongs thundered. Five enormous metal instruments stood in the training sands, facing the gate of the monastery. Monks frowned in fierce concentration as they stroked the reverberating metal in waves. Ari Ara's limbs shook. She had never been so close to the roar of the Spring Gate opening . . . even the Fanten would hear this deep in their root caverns, along with the hissing and groaning of melting ice, thundering river water, and the tumult of the High Mountain snowcaps breaking loose.

The moaning crashes of the Horns and Gongs swept through the crater valley of Monk's Hand down into Mari Valley. Shulen hollered in her ear that if the wind blew in the right direction, the faint echoes would be heard all the way to Mariana Capital.

Ari Ara shivered in delight at the unearthly cacophony. The five monks moved in fierce concentrated unison across the metal gongs. When they stopped, the last echo pulsed free from the metal and ran the circle of the valley before vanishing into the silence that remained.

Shulen spoke behind her. His voice sounded oddly flat after the enormity of sound.

"Now, we wait. If the Capital hears the Spring Gate open, they will send us a messenger hawk with their greetings."

Ari Ara glanced around. The monks, trainees, and orphans settled along the sun-warmed steps to keep vigil. At first, they waited quietly. Then murmurs and whispers broke out. As the hours passed, the talking fell off and all eyes scanned the horizon for first sight of the hawk. An orphan leapt to his feet, pointing in the wrong direction. With a laugh, a senior monk offered an impromptu geography lesson, demonstrating that most of Mariana lay to the northwest of the monastery.

Toward sunset, Ari Ara saw the messenger bird. She stayed silent, waiting to see if the farsighted orphan girl in front of her might snag the honor of first sight. She did, leaping to her feet with such delight that Ari Ara grinned, glad to have given her the chance.

The messenger hawk winged closer, gliding over the village and finally coming to land on Head Monk's outstretched arm. They waited breathlessly as Second Monk stepped forward, untied the tightly rolled parchment from the bird's leg, coaxed the hawk onto his own arm, and handed the scroll to Head Monk.

"Great Lady Brinelle and the nobles of Mariana Capital send greetings . . . they honor the arrival of spring . . . great festivals planned in the Capital for tomorrow . . . the Mari River is swollen with snowmelt . . . first plantings have begun in the south - "

Head Monk broke off. His eyes widened. His expression grew grave, but when he spoke again, he merely read the closing remarks.

"May the blessings of the ancestors fall upon us all."

The orphans and trainees cheered. Nobstick and Teapot Monk rounded them up to help prepare the feast. Ari Ara, however, kept her eye on Head Monk, and saw him bend to Shulen and whisper. The senior monks began to amble back to their chants. The warrior monks returned the Great Gongs to their storage rooms. Ari Ara quickly ducked out of sight of the kitchen monks, sliding into the shadows under the overhang as Shulen and Head Monk walked swiftly in the direction of the office. She hesitated less than a second before following. The two men slid the door shut, but the walls were thin. Hidden behind a pillar, Ari Ara crouched beside the crack under the door.

"This is very serious," Head Monk murmured.

"We suspected this might happen," Shulen replied wearily.

"But so soon?"

"It has been eleven years since . . . "

"Yes, yes, I know but, honestly," Head Monk sighed in frustration. "Again? War again? Have they no sense?"

"None," Shulen answered flatly. "The nobles of Mariana Capital have always profited from war while the common people pay the price in lost lives and orphans."

"Is there any possibility - "

"When Korin comes, we shall speak with him about stopping this foolishness, but I can make no promises."

Korin! Ari Ara silently mouthed in awe. *The Great Lady's son was coming here?*

"If we cannot sway him," Shulen stated with reluctance, "you know I must go -"

"Yes, yes, of course you must go. We hate to lose you after only six months, though."

Ari Ara's gut clenched.

"I, too, regret the timing, but as the Head of the Guard - "

"I understand, you must serve."

"No," Shulen objected, "if I go to Mariana Capital, it is not to win a war, but to stop it."

Ari Ara could sense the stunned silence of Head Monk.

"What good is it to teach *Azar* to one small girl, when I ought to follow the Third Brother's Way to stop the bloodlust and greed of those fools?"

"You will not be popular," Head Monk warned him. "They will kill you as surely as they tried to murder Alaren's descendants long ago!"

"Well, they did not succeed then and they will not succeed now. The nobles will find that I am not so easily killed," Shulen said with a chuckle. "The Desert King and all his warriors failed to put me in the grave; I doubt the soft-fleshed nobles will accomplish the task."

Their voices fell silent for a moment. In the half-shadows, Ari Ara trembled. They would try to kill Shulen for following *Azar?*

"It's insupportable," Shulen muttered. "The Desert King doesn't have the Lost Heir."

"You know - "

"Nothing more than you," Shulen quickly stated, "but I suspect that if Tahkan Shirar had his child, we would know about it by now."

"Perhaps that's what the nobles are after . . . trying to force his hand and reveal the Lost Heir," Head Monk mused.

Shulen made a disparaging noise.

"They don't care about the Lost Heir. They're just after the spoils of a war none of them will fight, but from which all of them hope to profit."

Ari Ara heard the sound of Shulen rising.

"What should we tell the others?" Head Monk asked.

"Nothing. We'll wait until Korin arrives."

Ari Ara heard footsteps and darted away before the door slid open.

CHAPTER NINETEEN

· · · · ·

Not a word passed her lips, but rumors flew through the monastery as if the news had wings. By nightfall, the monks spoke of nothing but the looming threat of war. The trainees gossiped breathlessly about the arrival of Great Lady Brinelle's son Korin. The youngest orphans ran around shouting and pretending to be the Lost Heir and Champion, fighting off imagined attackers. The spring air only fanned the flames of restless fever in their blood. Soon, a sparring round broke out as if the trainees could not wait for battle. Speculations about early spring Trials abounded. The orphans, awake long after their usual bedtime, jostled in fits of nerves and over-excitement.

Ari Ara sat on a bench feeling sick. She watched even the most serene monks fall into feverish discussions and arguments. It seemed she was the only person not eager for war, the only one besides Shulen who equated it with pain and misery and horror. She bit back tears and hugged her knees to her chest. The entire monastery had lost its mind.

For a week, her thoughts churned as muddy and agitated as the snowmelt flashfloods hurtling down the Monk's Tears River. Her dreams were filled with bleeding warriors and black rivers of bodies. In her worst nightmares, she ran through the rain and a slash of lightning revealed Shulen, sliced to bits and dying. She woke gasping, tangled in her blankets, heart hammering. Unable to sleep, she would lie motionless until dawn, then rise red-eyed and exhausted.

Each day turned darker than the next as the blight of looming war sucked the beauty of spring into withered blossoms of worry. Shulen spent more and more time with the warriors-in-training, finally cancelling his practices with Ari Ara. She rose on her own, miserable and lonely, and tried to dance *Azar* with the blustering wind. She couldn't focus and quit. Ari Ara climbed onto an ancestor pillar and watched the churning grey clouds hurtle overhead, trying to stay balanced as the rumble of war thunder pounded.

"Come."

Shulen's voice at her side startled her. His stony expression turned briefly to the sparring matches and grew harder.

"Let's go down to the river."

She jumped off the pillar and followed him at a half jog. The clatter of the monastery fell away. They walked down the path that splintered off toward the east. Just below the Fanten Forest, the river turned a fiercely tight corner over a tumble of boulders before widening across the long plateau of the lower meadows. Then it curled through the villagers' fields and out of Monk's Hand through the narrow pass where the Thumb and Forefinger cliffs drew close.

"Sometimes, Ari Ara," Shulen said quietly as they walked, "the world turns faster than you would like . . . and in a direction you fear and despise."

"Toward war," she muttered in disgust.

"Perhaps," Shulen conceded sadly. "And in any case, toward change, which is racing to Monk's Hand sooner than I would want. So, whether you're prepared or not, today is your Trial in *Azar.*"

"My what?!" she yelped, startled out of her moodiness.

"Your Trial," he repeated calmly. "There's only one way to test a true follower of *Azar.*"

Shulen walked to a spot where the river curled easefully through the trees.

"Can you swim?" he asked Ari Ara.

"Of course," she answered proudly.

"How well?"

"The fish will drown before I will."

"Good."

Without warning, he grabbed her and tossed her in the river.

Ari Ara shot back up to the surface, spluttering in surprise.

"What was that for?" she hollered over the rumble of the river, treading water against the pull of the current.

"*Azar* literally means *the way water flows between obstacles,*" he called back, pacing the bank as she was tugged downstream. "Today, kitten, you learn from the river. Follow her Way Between."

Ari Ara rolled her eyes and dove underwater. Submerged beneath the humming river, she swam along with the threading currents. She returned to the surface for air. Shulen watched silently, keeping even with her along the shore. Just before the river spilled out onto the plateau, he hollered for her to climb out.

She kicked over to the side and grasped his outstretched hand.

"Well?" he asked.

"Well what?" she answered, shaking water out of her eyes.

He sighed.

"Again."

He gestured for her to follow and began hiking back up the river through the trees. She sloshed along behind him. The day was hot and bright with a hint of the coming summer heat. The villagers could be seen planting in the fields across the bowl of Monk's Hand.

They reached the place where he first threw her in and before she could leap aside, he heaved her into the water. She spluttered and re-emerged, looking for Shulen. He wasn't paying any attention, simply strolling along the bank slowly, lost in thought. Irritated, she dove under again, into the dark rumble of the river. She held her breath as long as she could, allowing the current to twine around her torso and sweep her hair into spirals. Finally, she pushed off a submerged log and broke the gleaming surface.

Ari Ara drew a lungful of air and flipped over. She wove through the ripples of water streaming past her, twisting along with them. She rolled and spun, bumped into a rock, pushed off, and floated further. She returned for another gasp of air and sank back under. A thought struck her.

She splayed her fingers and felt the threads of faster water sliding through the slower currents. Cold seams rose off the dark bottom. A thin streak of warmth wavered near the surface. A crossroads of water split around a large boulder. She rode the left hand path, which shot her back into the crosscurrent on the other side. Ari Ara broke the surface for air and then dove to seek out the invisible roads of motion that carved and threaded through the river.

At the bend before the plateau, she swam toward the bank with quick, determined strokes. She scrambled up before Shulen reached out his hand, and took off running up the trail.

"Come on!" she called over her shoulder, her wet clothes whapping her limbs.

She dove in this time, fascinated. There *was* a Way Between the currents of the river. If one listened for it, watched for it, let the twining threads of water tell you where to go . . . there was a way to slide between the tumult and the tugging, and travel down an unseen path.

"Well?" Shulen said as she climbed out.

"It's there. I felt it," she panted. "Again!"

Shulen smiled and loped after her up the trail.

"Between the streams of water," she explained as she ran, "there's a way to move. If you follow that, the river guides you through her twists and turns."

"Yes!" Shulen agreed, leaping ahead of her, catching her midstride and tossing her back into the river in his exuberance. "Go find it!"

Ari Ara dove into the challenge. Again and again, she swam the long section of the river, faster and faster as she learned to sense the Way Between and let it propel her downstream.

"Enough," Shulen called out as the late afternoon sun relented and a touch of coolness arrived in the air. He hauled her out of the water. Ari Ara nodded. Her limbs felt as heavy as sodden tree roots. She watched the drips soak the sandy soil of the bank. Her reddened eyes glowed with happiness. She breathed deeply, then spread her fingers to see the extent of the wrinkles.

"Old monk's hands," she pointed out in a voice that cracked with weariness.

She rubbed the water out of her eyes and glanced tiredly at the long hike back up to the monastery. In the old days, she realized with a sigh, she would have just curled up right there on the bank, slept off her exhaustion, and started the day fresh from that spot. But times had changed. She was an apprentice now, not a wild mountain shepherdess. As Shulen gestured for her to follow, she picked up her feet and trudged up the trail.

"Did I pass my Trial?" she called after him.

Shulen laughed and turned back.

"Oh yes."

She had surpassed all of his expectations long ago, but there was no need to tell her that now. Being thrown in the river was a tradition, and a distraction from the black cloud of war. She would sleep solidly tonight without the nightmares he knew had been plaguing her.

Ari Ara grinned in exhausted delight.

"Come on, kitten," he said kindly. He took three steps toward her and scooped her up.

Surprise warred with exhaustion. Her aching muscles and sore lungs won. She wrapped her wiry arms around his neck and hung on, grateful for the warmth as the cool evening air flooded down from the peaks. Slowly, cautiously, she lowered her head until it rested on his shoulder. Her eyelids slid down toward her cheekbones.

So, this is what it's like, she thought, remembering how the village fathers sometimes carried the littlest children home from the festivals. She'd wondered, sometimes, when night fell and she had only her own tired feet to carry her back up into the mountains. Her head nestled sleepily. He walked in silence for a distance, through the trees and up the long rocky slope toward the monastery.

"We'll be there soon," he assured her.

No answer. She was already fast asleep.

CHAPTER TWENTY

. . . . .

She slept. Deeply. Profoundly. She dreamed of rivers of ancestor spirits. The black waters coursed across the star-laden night. She swam upstream and slid between generations of silver figures. Eons and epochs of time flowed past her. Fanten, Desert, and Marianan, all twisted into a great stream of life, entwined and overlapping. Ari Ara swam between them until she came to three towering figures: Marin, Shirar, and Alaren. The Third Brother stood between the others, wearing Shulen's wry expression.

She might have stood, awed and silent, for an eternity as the black river parted around them. But the Fanten Grandmother appeared, dressed in white and silver, dancing upstream through the currents. She startled at the sight of Ari Ara.

"What are you doing here?" she asked in a strangely realistic tone. She turned to the Three Brothers. "She shouldn't be here."

Ari Ara sighed. Even in dreams, she wound up in trouble.

Fanten Grandmother took her hand and was beginning to tug her back downstream when Alaren spoke.

"It's time."

The old woman craned over her shoulder and sniffed disdainfully. Ari Ara blinked. Not even Alaren could intimidate the silver-haired Fanten.

"No more secrets and hiding," Alaren told Fanten Grandmother, lifting a finger of admonition. Then, to Ari Ara's surprise, he pointed at her.

"Bring *Azar* back," Alaren told her gently.

"Enough!" Fanten Grandmother cried, glancing around at the black river of timelessness and the streams of ancestor spirits. "She should not be here!"

And she pulled Ari Ara downstream, even though the girl struggled to escape. A thousand questions burned on her lips, but when she called out, she swallowed the black river of souls...

... and woke up gasping for air.

The temple bell clanged. Footsteps treaded along the hallway as the senior monks rose from meditations and gathered for breakfast. Ari Ara's mind raced as fast as her heart.

The Fanten put great faith in their dreams, which they swore could foretell floods or coming births or gathering storms. In the official record of Shulen's Stand, it even noted that Fanten Grandmother, when asked how she knew where to send the Fanten to look for Shulen and the Queen, said that she saw it in a dream. The Fanten daughters were trained to remember their night journeys and as they grew, they learned to walk in each other's dreams as Fanten Grandmother had just done in hers. Ari Ara frowned in thought.

She had never dreamt such a vivid dream before. The Fanten said; the clearer the dream, the more significant it was. Ari Ara lay on her back, remembering the details. What had the Third Brother said, exactly? Bring *Azar* back.

Back where? she thought.

Then she sat up so fast she nearly hit her head on the shelf above her. Flinging back the sliding door, she spilled out directly onto a senior monk who was passing by.

"Oops, sorry," she apologized as she scrambled to her feet and sprinted down the corridor.

"Shulen!" she cried, skidding into the Main Hall. He was sitting at a table with Second Monk, his grey gaze clouded with worry. Ari Ara scrambled over the bench and sat next to him, breathless.

"Shulen, I had a dream."

"Not now, Ari Ara," he answered with a slight frown.

"It's important."

"Your dream?" Shulen replied with a short laugh.

"It was a Fanten dream," she emphasized.

That got his attention. He swiveled on the bench.

"A real Fanten dream?" he demanded sternly. His heart thudded in his chest. "They dream differently than lowlanders, you know. It's something in their blood."

"Well, no," she clarified, "at least, I don't think so. But, this was *like* a Fanten dream, vivid and powerful."

"Ah," he sighed, disappointed.

He turned back to his conversation with Second Monk. She tugged on his sleeve.

"Can it wait?" Shulen sighed. "There are things I need to - "

"I have to tell you!" she blurted out, louder than she intended.

The Main Hall fell silent for a moment. Shulen frowned. As the chatter cautiously resumed, he excused himself from Second Monk and gestured for Ari Ara to follow him.

"Come on then," he said, "tell me while I work."

He rose and brought his bowl over to the kitchen, then walked toward Head Monk's office.

"I dreamt I swam up the black river of ancestors - "

"Hardly surprising, given yesterday's immersion in the river," he pointed out.

"Yes, but then - "

She had to pause as he collected a set of messenger scrolls that had arrived in the night.

"Then, I met the Three Brothers and Alaren said - are you listening?"

Shulen glanced up from the scrolls with his eyebrows furrowed together.

"Alaren asked if you were listening? Were you?"

"No - "

"You weren't listening, how unusual," Shulen's mouth twitched in the corner.

"Shulen, that's not what I meant. Alaren said - "

She broke into a half trot as he suddenly strode off across the training sands.

"Alaren said it was time," she informed him, waiting expectantly for his reaction.

"Here," he replied, pulling a stack of poles and banners out of a closet. "Take those over to the landing."

Ari Ara gritted her teeth as he handed her the awkward armload, not bothering to ask about their purpose.

"So," she repeated to Shulen when she finished, "Alaren said it was time."

"Time for what?" Shulen asked absently, frowning at a pair of orphans who were fiddling with the pile.

"Time for *Azar*," Ari Ara answered. "It's time to bring it back."

"Back where?"

"Everywhere!" she cried, darting in front of him and hopping backwards as he went to chastise the orphans. "Alaren wants it brought out of hiding. No more secrets, he said. We have to bring it back to the people, the monks, the Capital - "

Shulen stopped short with a bark of bitter laughter.

"That's a dream, alright," he commented. He gazed out the gateway of Monk's Hand toward Mariana Capital.

"But what if it's a message and we're supposed to - "

"We?" Shulen raised an eyebrow.

"Yes, I could come to the Capital with you and - "

"No."

His voice was sharp.

"But - "

"You're not going to the Capital, Ari Ara."

"But the dream - "

"There's a war brewing!" he bellowed.

Heads turned at his roar. Ari Ara flinched. Shulen lowered his tone slightly. "It is absolute madness in the Capital right now. Every warrior is holding double training schedules in *Attar*. The blacksmiths are forging weapons around the clock. Thousands of people are pouring in from every corner of Mariana, some to fight, some to hide. You are not going to the Capital."

"But if we taught *Azar* - "

"Taught it to whom?" Shulen snapped.

"The warriors," Ari Ara answered, only realizing how odd it sounded once it was out of her mouth and lying awkwardly on the silent training sands of the monastery. "We could teach them the Way Between so they don't have to go to war."

"Better to teach the cursed nobles," Shulen muttered under his breath.

"Alright, them, too," she added, "and the Guard, the Heir's Champion, everyone. It's not just for fighting; it's for stopping conflicts before they start, like in the Third Brother's book."

Shulen heaved an exasperated sigh and sank down on his haunches in front of her. Monks and trainees were filing onto the training sands, waiting for practice to begin. He met her young eyes, so full of hope. She would not like what he had to say. Alaren's descendants had been murdered or forced into hiding for promoting *Azar* at a time like this. He supported her in principle, but it was dangerous at the Capital. Tempers would be running high. Mobs would hang suspected traitors and spies. She did not understand that it would be tantamount to political treason to argue against war once the nobles stoked the fever of the populace into eruption.

"Look, kitten, I'm not saying it isn't a good idea," he commented, holding up a hand for her to listen, not argue, "but this is not the time."

"Alaren said it was time," she muttered, feeling the pinprick of tears in her eyes.

"It was a dream, Ari Ara," Shulen told her firmly. "When the war is over - "

"Or stopped," she interrupted.

Shulen snorted.

"There's as much chance of stopping this war as there is of holding back the Mari River."

"But you said to Head Monk - "

She gulped as Shulen glared at her.

"You shouldn't be listening at keyholes," he growled.

She was in for it now, Ari Ara thought. She took a breath and plunged in deeper.

"You told Head Monk that there wasn't any point to teaching me if you weren't going to follow Alaren's Way yourself. You said you were going to go to the Capital to try to stop the war."

"That's right," Shulen confirmed coolly, "but never once did I say that a certain redheaded orphan was coming with me."

She opened her mouth to protest and he cut her off.

"The Capital is no place for you. Not right now. If the war preparations here disgust you," he swept his hand around the monastery, "what will you do in the Capital when the horror of the war breaks out in earnest? When the wounded roll in, missing arms and legs? When the orphans arrive wailing for their dead mothers? When pestilence rides the stench of death wafting from the border? You have never seen war. I have. And, I have no intention of letting you get near the screams of dying men, the black fields slick with spilled blood, the bodies writhing in all directions."

He spoke savagely, cruelly, knowing only harsh truth could keep her from following him.

"You will stay here in the High Mountains, far from torn limbs, eyes gouged out of sockets, women and children burned alive in their houses, tortured prisoners, and suspected spies hung in the streets by mobs."

"Stop!" she screeched, hating the look in his eyes. Shulen's hard greyness had turned to ice. His lips were white. His jaw clenched. He stared at her horrified face, noticing the Fanten way she curled her fingers into fists against her cheeks when frightened. Yes, he had seen that expression before. He had no desire to see it again. He swallowed hard, remembering.

He turned his back on the child. If pushing her away was the only way to protect her . . .

"Go climb the mountain," he ordered curtly. "I have warriors to train."

CHAPTER TWENTY-ONE

. . . . .

Ari Ara hurled a loose stone furiously at the blue sky. It wasn't her fault he wouldn't listen! She wasn't trying to throw herself into the middle of a war . . . she was trying to stop it! And you can't use *Azar* to disarm *Attar* if you're not willing to risk the dangers. The temple bell rang out below. Ari Ara glanced over her shoulder. As she ran off, Shulen had shouted after her to be back in time for . . . something . . . but the wind had swallowed the rest of his words. She shrugged. He probably meant chores or lessons. She refused to go study military maneuvers or polish shields and swords.

She took off running up the black heights. She climbed high enough to make the battle cries of *Attar* fade into the familiar song of the wind. Then she scaled a huge boulder, black with the sun and worn round with time. Ari Ara tucked her foot up onto her thigh and stood in her one-footed shepherdess pose, seeking balance for her madly racing heart. The wind hissed and moaned across the bowl of Monk's Hand, racing through the Fingers below. Shulen's harsh words rattled under her skin. The cruelty of his dismissal blistered her heart.

189

A thought nagged her, tenacious. She had the sense that they were all missing something as startlingly obvious as the blue of the sky. This was the challenge and the beauty of the Way Between: it wove through the world, right under everyone's short-sighted eyes, as commonplace as their own noses. *Azar* threaded between the wings of the birds and the winds of the mountains. *Azar* slipped between the tumbling water and the smooth stones of the river. *Azar* unfurled in the green young leaves budding on the trees and withered in the frost lines of autumn.

Attar roared into battle. *Anar* ran for cover. *Azar* stood its ground, neither causing harm nor allowing harm to be done. Neither fight nor flight, but a third option: a Way Between that brought the momentum of violence to the ground.

To the small child on the boulder overlooking the vast vista of the world, it was as simple as taking her next breath. If she could use *Azar* to stop Brol's attacks, then the Champions could use it to settle conflicts, the Guards could protect people with its strength, and the warriors could use it to stop invasions. She knew from the Third Brother's stories that *Azar* could be used from the smallest personal disputes to the largest conflicts brewing between nations. Shulen had spoken truly . . . the nobles should be studying *Azar,* and the villagers, the children, the monks, everyone.

Ari Ara's blue-grey eyes turned toward Mari Valley far off in the hazy distance. They had studied *Attar* for thousands of years, fighting wars, provoking, defending, battling, and glorifying the warriors while neglecting everything else. But they could change. Every hour she had spent listening to Scholar Monk drone on about wars and tactical maneuvers could be spent discussing the Third Brother's Way. They could learn how to stop wars from arising; how to address the causes of conflict and hatred; how to keep disputes from escalating into violence; how to air and address grievances; how to stand up to injustice; how to transform hearts and minds, and how to change enemies into friends.

Her thoughts drifted back to Brol. She had approached their conflict all wrong from the very beginning, she reflected pensively. She had fought with him, mocked him, laughed at him, ignored him, and humiliated him. She had seen Brol as her enemy because he was bigger and mean. *He hurt me*, Ari Ara thought bitterly, shaking her head to loosen the hot tears steaming in her eyes, *but I attacked him back, like the Marianans and the Desert People have been doing for a thousand years.*

What good did it do, really, to have bested him with *Azar*? He still glared at her resentfully, even if he didn't dare attack her anymore. She had become Shulen at his worst - tougher, faster, stronger than anyone else - but what did that solve? Nothing.

Ari Ara switched legs and continued brooding. Her eyes barely saw the verdant burst of spring sweeping across the crater valley. If she had truly mastered *Azar*, she would have taken that sweet roll to him and listened to him talk for hours. Then she'd have done it again. No matter what he said. No matter what he did. She could have used outer *Azar* to keep him from hurting her and inner *Azar* to shift his heart and mind so he no longer wanted to hurt her. Brol was walking around with a roaring battle under his skin. His memories, his pain, his past was wounding him every time he turned around. She thought about his snarl of a confession . . . that he should have been chosen to be Shulen's apprentice. In a strange way, she agreed. Brol needed *Azar*. Once, like her and Minli, he had also been

191

small and helpless, beaten and terrorized. He had turned to the warrior's way to protect himself and fight back.

But *Attar* was a cruel cycle of violence and fighting. It ended, ultimately, in death. *Attar* could hurt others before they hurt you . . . but it could never take away the hatred that drove people to fight. It bred more of it, feeding on cycles of violence, until *Attar* rose like a monstrous giant over the land, roaring and seemingly invincible, but without the power to help even the smallest wounds heal.

The sun climbed higher overhead. A hawk wheeled above her in slow, wide circles. *Bring Azar back,* Alaren had challenged her.

She never backed down from a challenge.

Shulen's stoney face rose in her memory, saying, "What if you lose?"

"You can't lose if you never give up," she had answered.

The words were as true now as they were on the first morning she had trained in *Azar.* Ari Ara laughed at herself and the impossibility of the task before her. Shulen had knocked her down in today's match of wills, she conceded, but she was back on her feet, clear-headed and determined, and she refused to give up until she succeeded.

She smiled into the bright winds of the Monk's Hand Mountains. She would find the Way Between the resistance of the Stone One. After all, *Azar* was the way water flows around obstacles without giving up.

She was deep in thought when the Horns sounded unexpectedly. The sun had shifted overhead; she'd been standing on the boulder for hours. Ari Ara squinted at the monastery, wondering what the racket was about. It wasn't the usual commemoration of the seasons and the only other time

192

the monks blew the Horns was on special occasions such as the arrival of visitors.

Her eyes flew open. She shaded the sun out of her gaze. Far below, tiny dots of grey-robed monks stood at the gates, waiting. Her gaze swept down the steps, through the village, all the way to the Thumb's Pass. Deep maroon welcome banners fluttered in the wind. Figures climbed the steps. An entire entourage of people approached. They were nearly halfway to the monastery. The villagers trailed behind them waving handkerchiefs and scarves wildly.

Korin! she realized with a gasp. The Great Lady's son must be arriving!

She took off down the boulders without bothering to watch her footing. *By the ancestors!* she swore. *That's what Shulen had wanted her back in time for!* She would be in so much trouble for missing the arrival. Her red hair streamed like a torch behind her. The Horns sounded and she heard the cheers of the monastery with them. Ari Ara altered her course. She couldn't burst in, hot and dirty, wearing her old training tunic with her patched pants held up with a length of old rope. She couldn't risk disgracing Shulen, not right now!

Ari Ara circled around the back of the monastery. She could pass over the roof, slip through the outer door near the orphans' quarters on the west side and sneak through the Main Hall to her cubbyhole. She'd change, splash some water on her face, and hopefully slide in among the assembled orphans and trainees before anyone realized she was missing.

Ari Ara climbed stealthily over the rocks to where the roofline reached the side of the mountain. She shoved her hair out of her eyes and began to pick her way across the tiles in a half-crouch. Over the top of the tiled roof, she heard voices. Ari Ara paused. Surely a peek wouldn't hurt . . . she gripped the mossy tiles and scrambled up. Carefully, she laid her belly flat on the sun-warmed length of the low sloping roof, and inched closer to the ridgepole. With just her eyes peering over, she took a long look at the scene below.

Monks, orphans, trainees, and villagers had all gathered to welcome Korin and his entourage. The Fanten Grandmother was not present. Ari Ara grinned. She didn't stand on anyone's ceremony but her own. There would probably be a celebration in the village later and the Fanten would undoubtedly make their appearance then.

The Great Lady Brinelle's son was a tall youth with a crop of curly blond hair and pale blue eyes. He looked young to Ari Ara, who never imagined the Great Ones as being beardless boys. Such illustrious figures stalked her imagination larger than life, semi-mythic and powerful, but here was a boy no older than Brol, though far more dignified, she decided.

Ari Ara rested her forearms over the ridgepole, feeling the warmth of the tiles on her ribs. Shulen stepped forward to welcome Korin with a deep bow of respect which the youth immediately pulled him from. He clasped the Stone One's hand and then gestured to another figure that stood quietly in the splendor of the Great One's entourage.

Emir Miresh.

Ari Ara bolted upright and nearly fell off the roof. She knew it had to be him. An electric tension emanated from his stance. He stood lightly on his feet, agile and lithe. He was a few inches taller than Korin, and, though they were nearly equal in build, there was a sheer strength to the fluid grace of Emir Miresh that made the well-built noble look almost willowy in comparison. She whistled softly under her breath. Emir Miresh, reigning champion of Mariana Capital, sworn to protect the royal family since the age of eight, grown into a legend at sixteen . . . he was here!

To Ari Ara's surprise, Shulen broke the formal handshake between student and master, and pulled Miresh into an embrace. The bottom dropped out of her stomach. A new sensation flooded her limbs. She gritted her teeth against the queasy, hot fire of jealousy as Shulen greeted Miresh like a son. Miresh said something to Shulen, and the older man turned with a ready smile on his lips. He threw an affectionate arm over the youth's shoulders. Ari Ara scowled. *No wonder Shulen doesn't mind leaving me here – he's got his close-to-son in the Capital already.*

He's mine! she thought ferociously, glaring at the black-haired youth.

At that instant, Shulen's eyes flicked up toward the roof.

Ari Ara ducked out of sight. She waited a few breaths then cautiously peeked out. Shulen was surreptitiously scanning the crater bowl with a frown as Head Monk introduced Korin to the senior monks. He's searching for me, Ari Ara realized and she dropped back behind the roofline.

Ari Ara counted to one hundred in slow, measured breaths, willing her temper to cool down below the boiling point. She closed her eyes and waited as the ceremony dragged on. When she heard the sound of people moving, she scrambled back up the tiles to the ridgepole. Peering over, she saw Shulen and Korin following Head Monk into the office . . . hopefully to discuss stopping the war.

Emir Miresh stepped forward onto the training sands and faced the palpably eager trainees. A gaggle of awestruck orphans darted behind the pillars of the overhangs, giggling in nervous excitement. Most of the inhabitants of the monastery and many of the villagers encircled the courtyard with an air of expectation.

Ari Ara appraised Miresh more closely. His blue-black hair was long, pulled into a tie at the back. His features ran fine, like many Marianans, thin nose, prominent cheekbones, and a sharp chin. There was something to the shape of his eyes that spoke of the northern hill-folk, the ones who lived in the edges of the Border Mountains. He was tall, more than half again her height, with a promise of breadth to his solid shoulders. The great Emir Miresh had not yet scratched the surface of his full potential, but he looked formidable enough now, she thought with a small shiver. What he lacked in girth and maturity, he gained in sheer energy and lithe grace.

A tiny orphan ran up, impetuously swinging at Miresh, mock sparring with him. He good-naturedly feinted from the child's efforts. Ari Ara felt a smile curling on her lips at the antics. She scooted up and threw her leg over the ridge, tired of clinging against the pull of the slope.

Miresh stopped the child with a gentle hold, ruffling his hair until the boy laughed. Then he nudged him back toward the other orphans and clapped his hands together for attention. Silence fell. Miresh strode to the center of the courtyard. Ari Ara leaned forward precariously to see which trainees were waiting under the overhang beneath her.

Then, unexpectedly, Miresh threw his head back and roared,

"Are there any warriors here?"

The temple bell boomed. Ari Ara grabbed her ears. The tile beneath her foot cracked. She slipped off-balance and skidded down the roof. She snatched at the rain gutter as she slid past, missed, and tumbled into the courtyard below.

CHAPTER TWENTY-TWO

. . . . .

She landed jarringly on her feet, but upright. Throwing her hair out of her eyes, she glared around boldly as if she had jumped, rather than fallen.

"You must be Shulen's apprentice," Miresh stated with a knowing expression and a twist of humor on his lips. Who else would attempt such an entrance?

He studied the wild creature as she scowled ferociously at him. He couldn't remember ever being so small and angle-edged. Her muscles ran in tight cords from calf to bicep. Her pointed chin tilted up defiantly. Her blue-grey eyes glinted with hard determination. A shock of unruly red hair fought loose from her bedraggled braid.

"So," he commented drily, "come to practice?"

"No," she replied casually, brushing off her sleeve, "just thought I'd drop by."

The assembly burst out laughing. The senior monks' wrinkled faces curled with knowing smiles as their eyes moved from Emir Miresh to their young troublemaker. The warrior monks leaned against pillars with arms crossed over chests, a mixture of amusement and sternness on their faces. One or two of the trainees - Brol among them - wore decided smirks as if hoping she was about to get into all the trouble she deserved. She could see Minli standing next to Teapot Monk. They bore matching, unsurprised expressions, indicating that they expected no less of a fiasco from her. She scowled at them.

"Fancy yourself the Heir's Champion, then?" Miresh asked, dropping his head with a small laugh. She was about to say no when his eyes leapt up with an undeniable glint of a challenge.

"As much as the next fool on the training grounds," she retorted.

The monks howled with laughter. Too late, she realized that Emir Miresh was the only other person standing in the packed sands of the training area.

To the side, she caught a glimpse of Minli groaning and grinning at the same time. She sighed inwardly; she'd never hear the end of this from him.

"Let's match," Emir Miresh said, almost casually.

She blinked. The courtyard grew silent.

"Wh-what?" she stammered.

"Shulen's apprentice," he said, "I challenge you to a match. You and me. Here. Now. Let's test your mettle."

Back down, one part of her mind ordered. *Do it*, another voice urged. A certain curiosity squirmed in her chest. She could never best Shulen . . . how long would she stand against Emir Miresh, who was rumored to be as great or even better than his teacher?

You won't have another chance, she told herself. Shulen would never let her or *Azar* stand Trial in the Capital, not formally. If she wanted to prove the Way Between could hold its own . . . now was the time.

She eyed Emir Miresh, reigning champion of *Attar*, trained in *Azar*, Shulen's only other apprentice. Alaren's words rumbled in her like echoes of thunder. A lightning-fast thought cracked through her. If she did well, maybe Miresh would help bring *Azar* back to the Capital!

The monks, trainees, and orphans waited breathlessly for her response.

"Agreed," she answered, throwing her braid over her shoulder with a touch of cheekiness. "We'll test your mettle, too."

A flurry of talk erupted. Miresh grinned. Nobstick and Teapot Monk started taking bets. The littlest orphans screeched in excitement. Minli smacked his forehead with his palm. She'd eat humble pie for this one. This wasn't Brol and the village boys . . . this was *the* Emir Miresh, champion of all Mariana.

The two stood stock still in the courtyard. Neither moved. Ari Ara watched for clues to his first move. The black-haired youth gazed at her with fierce concentration.

"I've heard you're quite a sight, Shulen's apprentice," Miresh commented. "Prove it."

She didn't move except to throw her head back with a contemptuous laugh.

"Proving is your task, not mine, Emir Miresh."

A smile curled across Miresh's lips - but it was not exactly friendly.

"You're no warrior, then, if you fear to strike first," he baited her.

"No," she answered calmly, "I am not a warrior."

Miresh glanced at her in surprise.

"Fear drives the first blow of all conflicts," she said haughtily, "and no one can call me a coward."

Emir Miresh laughed at this flame-haired child throwing Shulen's lines back in his face as if he hadn't heard them a thousand times.

Then he moved. Quicker than she expected - but not quick enough to catch her as she dove to the side! Miresh cursed silently. She was fast! Swift as a minnow in a stream, small and agile. They spun around each other. He had an easy throw of strength that could propel him halfway across the courtyard in a single leap. She noted that. His reach was nearly double hers and twice she missed the sting of his blows by a hair-ruffling fraction of a second. She dodged, using the openings he gave, not taking any risks.

"You can't defeat an opponent you never engage," Miresh taunted as she twisted away again.

Her smirk was the only answer.

Azar! he swore silently.

He watched her carefully. He had assumed that Shulen was training his apprentice in *Attar,* but no, Shulen had not trained her to fight. Her muscles sat all wrong. She did not react to return the attack. She simply wheeled around, leapt aside, and circled him, neither attacking nor disengaging, finding a Way Between his every move.

And the little minx was fast!

Every ounce of the creature was a sinewy band of muscle. She moved with her child's proportion of energy to mass. Emir Miresh switched his stance. He, too, had been thrown in the river. He, too, had stood in the wind. And he had five years of practice over the orphan!

The monks gasped when Miresh moved into the Way Between. Two rivers poured around one another. Form and emptiness danced. Shulen's apprentices moved heaven and earth in a sparring match of body and space. Ari Ara and Miresh flowed through holes in each other's motions. They rolled through openings in midair. They pushed the limits of human form. The edges of their limbs blurred as they evaded and turned.

A hush fell over the courtyard. Monks, trainees, and orphans sensed something rare and record-worthy was unfolding before their eyes. Legends would grow from this encounter of two apprentices, trained by the same master, the elder testing the younger.

Ari Ara and Miresh no longer sparred; they danced in sheer astonishment with one another. *Azar* pulled the rivalry from their hearts, weaving a bond of surprised respect in its place. As their grudge dissolved, their motions shifted from defensive to luxurious. Her limbs flew in wide arcs. His long reach spiraled. She back-flipped into a glorious sweep over his dive. No one breathed in the ranks of the observers. Miresh drew her out, turning his motions into invitations that evoked the Fanten in the gestures of the girl. She slipped into half-trance. He saw it, noted it, gathered his speed, let her move into a series of spins, whirls, rolls, and a leap that dropped the mouths of the monks.

Then Miresh made his move. He lunged into a spring. Midair, he grasped her waist and pulled her out of the dance and into the fight!

Ari Ara roared at the betrayal. She flung the counterweight of her small body to twist the momentum of his leap off-balance, levered his mass under her, rebounded jarringly off the sands, and, using *Azar* against *Attar*, twisted her torso and . . .

. . . pinned her knee against his throat.

A shocked gasp shot across the courtyard. The angular orphan leaned over the great Champion. Miresh slowly moved his hands above his head in the gesture of surrender.

"Just what," said a stern voice behind her, "are you two doing?"

Ari Ara spun.

Shulen stood above them sterner than she had ever seen . . . though the twitch in the corner of his mouth betrayed him.

"Help him up," Shulen ordered her.

Ari Ara flushed and extended her hand to Miresh. He clasped it good-naturedly and allowed her to pull him to his feet.

They stood before Shulen as sheepish as any pair of apprentices caught in an illicit sparring match. But before his wrath could fall, someone - Ari Ara suspected Minli - let loose a whoop of enthusiasm and the courtyard erupted in a cacophony of cheers.

Shulen blinked in surprise and glanced around as if noticing the packed courtyard for the first time. The senior monks were standing under the eaves. The trainees raised their hands in salute on the edges of the sands. The orphans leapt up and down in wild enthusiasm. A slow grin rose in Shulen's stern expression. He clasped each of his apprentices on the shoulder. Ari Ara could see the edges of his eyes folding in mirth even as he tried to scowl at them.

"Emir, you need to guard your back in turns," he scolded, "and Ari Ara, what were you thinking, letting yourself fall into a Fanten trance?!"

She exchanged a quick conspiratorial glance with Miresh before ducking her head dutifully at the critique.

"Alright, the lot of you," Shulen hollered at the crowd, "get to your practices. Enough excitement for one evening."

His grip tightened on Ari Ara's shoulder. She gulped. She wasn't out of hot water yet! Shulen barked out instructions to Second Monk, then muttered to her,

"To my quarters now." He turned to Miresh. "If you would join us . . . "

His hand on Ari Ara did not loosen as they threaded through the crowd. Many of the monks patted her on the head as she passed. Miresh accepted their jibes in good humor, saying it was an honor to lose to an apprentice such as this.

It was Korin's remark that set Ari Ara's heart racing.

"Outstanding! Why, we've found the Lost Heir's Champion!"

Ari Ara's eyes widened at the thought. She shot a look at Shulen as if to say, *See? I'm going to the Capital whether you like it or not.* Shulen gave her a hard glare in response and shook his head.

"That is high praise, Korin," Shulen replied, "but Ari Ara will not be Champion to the Lost Heir."

"Well, the Guard then, at any rate," Korin enthused.

"I think not," Shulen answered grimly.

Ari Ara opened her mouth to protest, but Shulen ignored her. He invited Korin to join them in his quarters.

When they reached the small room, Shulen gave her a little push to stop her from dragging her feet.

"In," he commanded.

She sat in her usual spot, arms crossed over her chest. Korin and Miresh lowered themselves onto the cushions. Shulen took his seat.

Ari Ara glowered at him. Why was he always like this? He ought to be celebrating, not scolding! It wasn't every day that one beat the reigning champion of Mariana with *Azar!*

Emir Miresh echoed her sentiments.

"What's this about not letting her join the Guard, Shulen? She's a natural. If she's this good now, she'll be a legend by sixteen."

Shulen drummed his fingers on the low table.

"That is unlikely to be Ari Ara's path," he said cryptically.

203

"Whyever not?" Korin exclaimed. "We've been saying for years that we need more women in the Guard. Even Mother herself - "

" - has sufficed with male guards as have many of the previous royal ladies. I did not train Ari Ara to serve Mariana's royalty."

"Then why train her at all?" Miresh asked with a frown.

Shulen sighed.

"For her sake. For mine. To prove the unproven potential of *Azar*."

"Well, she's certainly done that!" Korin commented enthusiastically. "When the rumor of this match reaches Mariana Capital, every warrior worth his salt is going to want to train in the Way Between!"

Ari Ara grinned. Shulen shook his head.

"The Way Between is not for warriors. They will seek to use it to further their victories in *Attar* . . . but that is not the Way Between." Shulen soberly regarded Miresh and Ari Ara. "That is why she was able to best you tonight, Emir. I trained you first in *Attar*. Ari Ara, on the other hand, has lived and breathed only *Azar*. And, the Way Between, even wielded by the least skilled, but most sincere-hearted, will always best the fighters trained in *Attar*."

"She's hardly the least skilled," Miresh quietly pointed out in the girl's defense.

"Ari Ara's skill ended when she accepted your challenge," Shulen said coolly.

Ari Ara opened her mouth to protest then shut it angrily. Hot tears threatened in the corners of her eyes. It was so unfair!

"She's a child, Shulen," Miresh said gently as the older man's stony grey eyes locked with the girl's in a battle of wills.

"Would you take her life from her, Emir Miresh?" Shulen answered without looking away from Ari Ara. "Would you take her life away in service in the Guard? As yours was taken at eight years old? As mine was at ten?"

Emir Miresh's eyes narrowed. Shulen's expression ached with brutal compassion. His heart tore in pieces from conflicting emotions, pride on the one hand, concern on the other; a thrill of excitement for the match he had just witnessed; a shiver of fear for the girl; memories of his past - losses, sacrifices, failures, disasters - and projections of the hardships endured by the Guard. He did not wish that life on many, and especially not on her, this girl who had found the Way Between the stone armor of his heart. He had taken her as his apprentice, but he would not condemn her to follow him into the sorrow of his path.

"Let her have her life, Emir. Let her fall in love someday, have children, grow old with the ones she loves. Don't make her sacrifice all that in service of the royalty of Mariana."

"What if I want to?" Ari Ara shot back, her blue-grey eyes flashing. "What if I don't want to stay here in Monk's Hand?"

"We've spoken about this," Shulen warned her sternly.

Ari Ara made a disparaging sound and tossed her head rebelliously. Shulen scowled. The gesture reminded him strongly of her earlier, wild habits when she first came to the monastery.

"You can't tell me what to do," she snapped at him.

"You are my apprentice," he retorted.

Miresh and Korin watched in surprise as they argued.

"Only until you leave," she spat back. "Then I'm Ari Ara of the High Mountains again, nobody's orphan, beholden to no one's command. I go where I please and I do what I want. I could walk through the Thumb's Pass, right down to the Capital, and apply to the Guard, and you can't stop me!"

"Yes, I can," Shulen answered calmly.

"Just you wait and see, Shulen!" she flared at him. "I'll prove I can."

"I don't think so, kitten," he chuckled, reaching out to tap her nose in affection.

She slapped his hand away. His grey eyes turned hard.

"Those who serve in the Guard must be nominated by the Head of the Guard," Shulen informed her without mercy. "And I will not be putting your name forward."

Ari Ara's temper boiled. Before they could stop her, she leapt to her feet and bolted from the room, shooting down the corridor and out of the monastery. She raced back toward the high peaks, out of reach of them all!

CHAPTER TWENTY-THREE

· · · · ·

She leapt boulders in a pounding stride, legs burning, her heart boiling with frustration at Shulen. What more could she do to convince him to bring back *Azar*? She'd just demonstrated its strength; he couldn't deny the hard truth of what he had seen. Ari Ara kicked a dry clump of last year's brown grasses as she ran past. Her chest heaved in the cool spring air.

Temper, temper, she chided herself, gripping the heat of her anger inside her chest like a burning iron brand. It writhed and singed until she roared with fury and let it out in hot yells that scorched the evening.

Even Shulen knew the war had to be stopped, she thought ferociously. He told Head Monk that he would go the Capital and risk death to use *Azar* to -

She froze. Her heart thudded as a sudden realization pounded into her stubborn head. Tears stabbed her eyes. He'd said it over and over.

It wasn't that he wouldn't bring *Azar* to the Capital.

It was her.

"Stupid. Stupid. Stupid." She spat the words out bitterly. Her voice sounded harsh in her own ears. How could she be so blind? Ari Ara's cheeks turned red in fury. *I was just . . .* she choked . . . *an amusement. A game to relieve the boredom of Monk's Hand.*

The old tiger just wanted a kitten to tease.

Ari Ara bared her teeth in a silent hiss of anger.

She heard the mocking scorn of memories leaping back at her. Her mind echoed the thousand slights and insults from her life. No one wanted her. The village boys threw stones at her. The monks chased her out years ago. The Fanten excluded her from their ceremonies. Ari Ara. Not this. Not that. You don't belong here, they'd said. We won't accept you into the Guard. You can't come to the Capital. You aren't allowed to live in the village. You can't stay with the Fanten over the winter.

Ari Ara scooped up a stone and hurled it at a boulder. No matter how hard she tried. No matter what she did. She never belonged anywhere. Not with the warrior monks. Not with the Fanten. Not with anyone.

"Fine!" she hollered into the distance. "I'll just stay here. I can live in the mountains. I've done it before."

She blinked back tears as she looked at the foreboding black stones of the High Mountains. She had lived through that one winter . . . half of it, anyway . . . and just barely. But back then, she hadn't known the warmth of the monastery fires, or the joy of listening to their Feast Day songs, or had a friend like Minli, or known the fun of the games, or trained with . . . she cut off the thought of Shulen. It would be a thousand times lonelier in the High Mountains now, knowing what she was missing amidst the silence and space.

"You should never have taken me in!" she hollered in the direction of the monastery. And, because it was too far away for anyone to hear, she screamed at Shulen, "I should never have trusted you!"

The sky swallowed the sound. The wind blew hollow moans across the steep slopes. Ari Ara felt cold moisture running down her cheeks. She ran onward.

In the cold, high section of the Monk's Tears River, deep in the curve of the Fingers where only the mysterious Fanten ventured, Ari Ara splashed water on her face and scrubbed her skin clean of the grit of her anger. The cold water stole her heat away, leaving her shivering and feeling empty inside.

Ari Ara stood for a long moment, uncertain. The rumble of the river flowed past her along with the hiss of the wind through the glossy boughs of the trees. Every inch of the land felt ancient and still, carved with time and quiet. Not even the endless wars of the lowlanders could disturb it.

Ari Ara's face scrunched in disgust. If it wasn't for war, Shulen wouldn't be keeping her from the Capital . . . he wouldn't even be going away. He'd be staying at Monk's Hand for the whole year. She wished they would find the Lost Heir already and stop the stupid war . . . Ari Ara's eyes widened. Her mouth fell open. That was it!

In a flash, she was on her feet, racing into the depths of the Fanten Forest.

CHAPTER TWENTY-FOUR

. . . . .

Her red hair flung behind her as she darted down the nearly invisible footpath through the great towering trunks of the trees. In her mind, three thoughts repeated: find the Fanten Grandmother . . . ask her to reveal the Lost Heir . . . stop the war.

It was so simple, Ari Ara nearly laughed out loud. The old woman would tell her exactly where the Lost Heir was hidden - as soon as Ari Ara told her about the war! Fanten hated violence and warmongering. The older women hissed that it left the taste of metal on their tongues just to speak of it. Ari Ara had heard their scornful discussions hundreds of times. They warned their daughters not to be like the lowlanders, always fighting among themselves. *Watch your temper,* they'd tell the girls, *or you'll end up killing each other like those fools in the deserts and valleys.*

Finding the Fanten, however, was easier said than done. Ari Ara followed all the familiar footpaths without catching a single glimpse of them. She wove through the shelters under the Great Trees. No one. She stopped in the mossy grove and turned in a circle, pondering.

If they didn't want to be seen, not even a Fanten daughter could find her own mother in the forest. The Fanten version of hide-and-seek could last for weeks. Ari Ara bit her lip. *There must be a way*, she thought desperately. Her eyes darted between the reddish trunks of the trees. She sensed the Fanten's eyes on her and suspected they were close. A twig cracked. She whirled. No one.

They're here, Ari Ara thought firmly. *I know they are.*

Without thinking, she slipped into *Azar*'s inner way of seeing and gazed around the grove of enormous trees. She looked between the trunks and shadows, seeking what was not visible.

And there they were.

In the branches, leaning against the trunks, sitting under the roots, crouched behind boulders; the Fanten were hidden in plain sight, cloaked in shadows and secrecy. The Fanten Grandmother stepped forward.

"Well done," she said approvingly.

Ari Ara realized with a start that she must have grown over the winter; her eyes were level with the old woman's dark gaze.

"I came to ask you - to tell you - there's going to be war in the lowlands."

The diminutive, powerful woman did not look surprised at the news.

"Unless they find the Lost Heir, that is," Ari Ara added breathlessly.

The Fanten Grandmother smiled slightly.

Ari Ara took a breath and continued.

"Do you know where the Lost Heir is?" she asked boldly.

"Yes, of course."

The Fanten laughed.

Ari Ara glanced sideways and bit back her irritation at the sight of their smirks, sensing that they all knew a secret she did not.

"Will you tell me?" she asked the Fanten Grandmother. "Please? It would stop the war."

To her surprise, Fanten Grandmother shook her head.

"Let the lowlanders kill each other," she said in disgust.

"How can you say that?!" Ari Ara shot back.

The Fanten in the trees stirred uneasily. Angry undertones hummed through the shadows at the girl's defiant attitude.

"All those people! Fathers, mothers, sons, daughters! Dead, because you won't give up one of your miserly secrets!" Ari Ara continued in an accusatory tone.

The undertone rose to an audible rumble of disapproval.

Fanten Grandmother's expression turned to stern. Ari Ara tried another tactic.

"Please, if it were your own daughter - "

"You trespass on secrets you know nothing about," Fanten Grandmother hissed angrily at her. "My daughter is dead, murdered for meddling with warriors and heirs."

Ari Ara gulped at the white fury blazing in the old woman's dark eyes. Ari Ara swallowed and steeled herself. She had to keep trying.

"You know where the Lost Heir is," Ari Ara accused, "and you're just sitting on the knowledge when you could use it to stop not just this war, but all wars."

Ari Ara stared steadily at the Fanten Grandmother, thinking of the dream and wondering if the woman remembered. She could see the wrinkles in the corners of the elder's eyes twitching with rapid thoughts. Ari Ara spoke swiftly, pressing her point.

"I saw you in my dream, dancing up the black river of the ancestors. You were there. You heard Alaren," she said. "Bring back *Azar,* he said. It can be done and it could stop them from fighting more wars. But we need time, and for that, we need the Lost Heir."

Fanten Grandmother's eyes widened.

Aha! Ari Ara thought. *So she did remember the dream!*

"The time is now," she said, quoting Alaren. "No more secrets and hiding. He was talking to you when he said that."

Fanten Grandmother's eyes narrowed, caught in a trap she didn't like. The eyes of the Fanten were pinned on their headwoman. To deny a dream shared by another was unthinkable. Fanten Grandmother crossed her arms over her chest and lifted a white eyebrow.

"Think you're clever, are you?" she mocked.

Ari Ara felt an uneasy lurch in her stomach.

"Let's strike a bargain," the silver-haired woman suggested with a gleam in her eye.

Ari Ara gulped. A Fanten bargain? Those were dangerous. She remembered the stories they told of tricking lowlanders with their clever ways. The Fanten loved to fool the unsuspecting into giving up something they didn't wish to exchange. Ari Ara didn't like the idea, and said as much.

"Ah, but you could stop a war," Fanten Grandmother coaxed, repeating her words back to her. "Think of all those lives saved and all the orphans spared the loss of their parents."

The girl frowned.

"I don't have anything to exchange," Ari Ara protested. "Unless you want me to watch the sheep again?"

Fanten Grandmother waved her hand dismissively.

"No, those days are done."

She stepped back a pace and eyed the redheaded girl. In the trees, the gazes of the Fanten assembly turned toward Ari Ara. Fanten Grandmother pursed her lips, tapped her chin, then spoke.

"You have something we want back."

Ari Ara's knees shook slightly. What could it be? From the gleam in Fanten Grandmother's eyes, it was something important.

"What?" she asked nervously.

Fanten Grandmother drew herself up to her full height.

"*Azar*," she answered.

Ari Ara's mouth fell open.

"Alaren said it," Fanten Grandmother reminded her. "Bring *Azar* back . . . back into the Hundred Sacred Dances, back to the Fanten from whom it originally came. We dance tonight for the Marianan Great One," Fanten Grandmother informed her. "We want you to perform with us . . . and dance the Way Between."

"But I haven't danced with the Fanten in years," Ari Ara stammered, flustered, "not since I was very small, and never in public before!"

Fanten Grandmother waved her objections aside like gnats.

"This is my offer," she stated firmly. "You dance *Azar*. We reveal the Lost Heir."

She pinned the girl with a fierce look.

"Do you accept?"

Ari Ara met the grandmother's eyes. She never turned down a challenge.

"Yes," she answered. "I accept."

CHAPTER TWENTY-FIVE

. . . . .

Ari Ara walked tall in the line of Fanten women descending from the dark towering forest toward the village. She held her head high, determined to uphold her end of the bargain. Her stomach fluttered with nervousness. In front of her walked the woman who danced the Water, the grandmother who moved in the gestures of the Wind, the daughter who portrayed the Sun. Every Fanten knew the Hundred Sacred Dances - or rather, the ninety-nine that remained after *Azar* was lost - but as they matured, each Fanten specialized in one dance. On rare occasions, they gathered like tonight to dance the web of the Hundred Sacred Dances. There was Deer and Wolf and Bear; Fern, Moss, Lichen; Stone, Snow, Ice; and Birth and Death, the great pair. Each role contained ritual elements, but each dancing was an improvisation created by the dancer.

Behind the long line of dancers came the drummers carrying their instruments strapped on their backs. Some of the drums were nearly as tall as the Fanten women. They descended from the forest toward the village in a long procession that made the breath catch in the throats of those who saw them coming. Even Ari Ara had never seen so many of the elusive

Fanten assembled in one place. Women and girls had been arriving in the grove all afternoon, coming down out of the forests. Some had even come from the mountains further beyond Monk's Hand. They brought greetings from the Fanten men and word of the summer gatherings later in the year. Ari Ara had watched it all in awe. The distant Fanten wore cloaks and dresses such as she had never seen. Their dialect of Fanten Tongue was difficult to follow. She knew thousands of Fanten lived along the high rim of the mountains that bordered Mari Valley, but she had never seen travelers from those places. Usually, the Fanten from Monk's Hand went to visit, and Ari Ara was never invited to go.

Every Fanten tonight - young and old - wore their ceremonial dresses. Their long dark hair was swept up into braided crowns atop their heads. For jewelry they wore gleaming polished wooden beads carved from the fallen branches of the Great Trees. The intricately carved beads dangled from fine blue threads that had been spun from the whitest fleece of the most ancient sheep and dyed with a secret root that only a few Fanten elders knew. Their dresses opened at the back and flared into full skirts at the bottom. The Fanten Grandmother wore a pure white, generations-old dress handed down from one headwoman to another. A few silver dresses dotted the line of women. Most wore the pure black of the Fanten sheep . . . and none had on anything like Ari Ara's dress.

The Fanten Grandmother had taken her into one of the deep caverns beneath the Great Trees and brought forth a bundle of cloth.

"You will wear this," she commanded and shook loose the garment in her arms.

218

It was a dress, Fanten style in its cut, open at the back, full in the skirt, but made of a shimmering fabric that did not come from the sheep's backs.

"That's not Fanten!" Ari Ara gasped.

"It is Desert silk in a Marianan weave, cut to a Fanten pattern, " the old woman replied. "Not this, not that. Like you."

"Where did you get it?" Ari Ara whispered, hardly daring to breathe.

"No questions," she replied in a typically infuriating Fanten way.

Now, the silver-white dress with thin threads of gold swung around her ankles as they entered the village. Her hair was braided and pinned around her head. A few tendrils rebelliously worked free and tickled her bare shoulders. She shivered slightly as the night air ran down her back. She had never worn anything like this dress before. She felt odd in her own skin . . . and yet, powerful, too. A sense of possibility crackled around her. Anything could happen tonight.

Where was that girl? Shulen had combed the monastery looking for her, searching the small sands between the boulders, opening cupboards and broom closets, scanning the darkening heights for the distant spark of her red hair. He had lingered behind while everyone descended to the celebration in the village to honor Korin's arrival. As the monastery grew empty and still, he searched. Shulen scowled. He wanted to have a quiet talk with the girl, to explain so many things he had not had a chance to say. Change was moving swiftly these days. He needed more time. He looked in the back storerooms and through the shelves of the archives. Nothing.

Drat her! The girl was just like the Fanten - impossible to find. For the hundredth time, he wondered at her bloodlines.

She claimed she was not Fanten, and could not sleep the Fanten sleep, and yet . . . if her dream of Alaren had been an actual Fanten dream . . . Shulen's heart quickened. He strode back through the senior monks' corridor. If he found the girl, he would tell her, finally, after all these months, the impossible thought that plagued him. For if she was part Fanten, then there was no question who she must be.

Shulen paced out across the courtyard and to the landing. He paused at the top of the long stairs and shouted her name. His voice bounced off the empty monastery walls and echoed up the mountains. *Ari Ara,* the stones called back. *Not this. Not that.* Shulen sighed. He shook his head, scanned the dark slopes again, then turned and climbed down the stone steps.

The Fanten dancing had already started when he reached the village center. The throbbing drums and eerie trills rang out in the deepening night. As he approached, he could see their figures leaping and whirling to the rhythms. The familiar ache of old sorrows tugged his heart. He set his face into stone to hide his regrets. Across the crowd, he could see Korin seated to the side and Emir standing behind him. The crowd cheered exuberantly and whistled at the energetic dancing.

A tight knot of shoulders blocked his way. Impatient, he craned to see beyond them. In the intricate weaving improvisation of a hundred whirling Fanten women, a streak of red hair caught his eye. The motion startled him with familiarity. Slowly, comprehension dawned. His jaw dropped at the sight of the shimmering child dancing *Azar* among the spinning Fanten. Shulen slid between the shoulders and backs. He subtly nudged bodies out of his path as if parting tall grasses in a summer field. In the front, Ari Ara danced with every ounce of her wiry strength. Her motions flowed in the unmistakable patterns of *Azar* while the beat of the drums evoked the Fanten in her gestures.

The old warrior walked closer. Shulen frowned as he approached Korin and Miresh. The two youths wore identical expressions of shocked disbelief: mouths open, eyes wide, surprise etched in every line of their faces. Shulen followed their gazes to the girl. It was only then that he saw the black mark between her shoulder blades; only then that he recognized the white dress for what it was; only then that he realized the reason for the youths' stunned faces.

"Oh ancestors, Ari Ara," he groaned. How could he have been so blind? He clutched the nearest shoulder for support as his heart leapt and crashed at the same time. His secret hopes shattered at the sight of the black mark, and his long years of searching came to an end.

In the torchlight, oblivious, Ari Ara whirled between the graceful motions of the Fanten, half-blinded by the lights and the sheer joy of the dance. She was in ecstasy, in Fanten trance. For once in her life, she belonged. Not this, not that, but everything possible in between. She could sense the throb of the drums in her bones and the trills ringing in her veins. She was born for this, to dance *Azar,* to bring it back as Alaren wished, to use the Way Between to bring peace among the warring factions.

This! she thought. This was how *Azar* was meant to be expressed - not as a fight or a match, but surrounded by community as one dance within the web of all other dances. The Fanten women swirled like the forest, wind, river, rain, and snow. Since ancient times, they had danced these elemental beings . . . and now she had returned *Azar* to the sacred dances, weaving the Way Between.

In the whirl of everyone, Ari Ara felt the impossible dissolve into the unlimited potential of the Way Between. All possibilities pulsed in her blood. The winding river of her life leapt and twisted before her. She did not need Shulen to follow *Azar* down into Mari Valley, into the Capital, to the Border Mountains, to the Desert! She would make her own Way Between. She belonged to no one, and to everyone. The Third Brother had chosen her to bring *Azar* back into the dance.

The speed of the drums quickened. Ari Ara doubled her pace. The onlookers gasped as she leapt around one Fanten and arched over another. Hands joined with the drumbeats, clapping to the inconceivable rhythm. She laughed with the sheer joy of the movement. The thunder of the beats peaked. The connection of dancers and drummers pulsed. Then abruptly . . . everyone stopped.

Ari Ara stood, wordless, as the resounding silence hung over the entire crowd. The Fanten Grandmother met her eyes across the circle. The crowd erupted. Trills, cheers, whistles, the stamp of appreciative feet pounding, and the clatter of hundreds of clapping hands flooded the village center. The Fanten Grandmother came over to her and clasped her hand.

"The Fanten thank you for returning the Way Between to the dance . . . and we release you to follow your path."

Ari Ara blinked at the odd turn of phrase.

She began to ask what the woman meant, but suddenly Shulen stepped in front of her. His face was lined with worry and strange emotions that she could not interpret. He put his hand on her shoulder.

"Ari Ara," he sighed, "you may not like what you have just become."

Whatever did he mean? she thought, annoyed at his cryptic remark.

His hand shot out and gripped her wrist with a stone-like strength. Fanten Grandmother grasped her other. The two exchanged a weighted look. Then Shulen lifted his free hand for silence. Ari Ara frowned at the stunned expressions on Korin and Miresh's faces. What was the matter with everyone?

Shulen nodded to the tiny, silver-haired woman, indicating that she should speak.

"Great One," Fanten Grandmother said solemnly to Korin, "allow me to present Ari Ara of Monk's Hand, raised by the Fanten and the High Mountains, trained in *Azar* under Shulen's guidance, and, by the weight of the Prophecy and the Mark of Peace that lies between her shoulders . . . the Lost Heir of two lineages, next to inherit the thrones of King Tahkan of the Desert and Queen Alinore of Mariana."

CHAPTER TWENTY-SIX

. . . . .

Thunderstruck shock burst across the crowd. The ground heaved beneath Ari Ara's feet. A cacophony of sound exploded from all sides, shouts of surprise, awed questions, rapid whispers, wild cheers. Shulen held her wrist in a firm grip as her knees buckled.

Korin came striding toward them, turning Ari Ara around and pointing at her back. Miresh joined him with surprise hanging on every corner of his face. She craned her neck to see the Mark, but couldn't, of course. The Fanten Grandmother stood calm and composed amidst the commotion, the smallest hint of a smile on her lips. Orphans squeezed closer, bumping and pointing at the Mark between her shoulder blades. Head Monk appeared, breathless and gasping.

"Ari Ara? The Lost Heir?"

He spun her around to verify the sight of the Mark.

"The Mark of Peace . . . we never checked," he muttered weakly. "We check all our orphans, but - "

"She was never *your* orphan."

The Fanten Grandmother spoke firmly. Her silver hair gleamed under the torchlights. She stood regal in her ceremonial dress, defiant and sovereign.

Ari Ara looked from one somber face to the next. The urge to run struck her.

"Don't," Shulen ordered softly, guessing at the twitch of her limbs.

"The Lost Heir . . . this whole time . . . you knew?" Head Monk stammered to the small, powerful woman.

"Yes," Fanten Grandmother replied, implacable.

"But you let her grow up among the sheep!" Head Monk cried.

"Fanten sheep have better hearts than most lowlanders," the silver-haired woman spat out, contemptuous. "I came to your monastery when the child was young, but you fools were already at each other's throats."

"You could have stopped the War of Retribution!" Head Monk protested. "Simply by handing the child over - "

"Humph!" she snorted. "And that would have started a dozen Wars of Reclamation as you all fought for control of the Heir. Better to let her grow up among the Fanten sheep than surrounded by such nonsense."

"There will be more wars," Shulen sighed, weary of the inevitable.

"Not with a Fanten-raised, *Azar*-trained heir on both thrones," she countered.

"Did she have any idea?" Korin asked, curious.

"No," Ari Ara and Fanten Grandmother, together.

"None," Shulen confirmed in an odd voice.

"Did you know?" Korin asked, eyeing the grey-haired man suspiciously.

Shulen shook his head.

"No. I thought . . . " he trailed off, but said nothing more.

Ari Ara caught a gleam in Fanten Grandmother's eyes as she studied Shulen's expression. More secrets, she suspected. The noise of the crowd subsided as the villagers and monks nudged each other into silence, pointing and whispering.

"How did you come by Queen Alinore's dress?" Shulen asked the old woman.

"She wrapped the child in it and handed it to me."

"What?!" Head Monk spluttered. "But you said the child wasn't there when the Fanten found the Queen."

"She wasn't," Fanten Grandmother replied calmly. "When the other Fanten got there, I had already taken the child."

Surprise rippled through the crowd. Mutters broke out. Fanten Grandmother lifted her hand imperiously for silence.

"Here is what I will tell you now," Fanten Grandmother informed them haughtily. "It was I who first found Queen Alinore, alive and laboring to deliver her child. In the night, my daughter had come to me in a dream, begging for help. She was attendant to the Queen, emissary of the Fanten. When the Queen fled from her attackers, it was my daughter who tried to get her to safety in the forests here."

Shulen's eyes clouded and Ari Ara realized with a jolt of surprise that he must have known the Fanten daughter . . . perhaps that had been the spirit she had seen on the night she followed him into the ravine.

"Lowlanders do not dream as Fanten do. Our blood sings in the ancient ways of this land and when our daughters cry to us in our sleep, we come to them. I flew on the wind and rode the mists, but even then I was too late. I arrived in time to help, but not soon enough to save . . . " Fanten Grandmother bowed her head to acknowledge the sorrow of her failure. "My daughter had hidden the young Queen in the safety of the Fanten cave beneath the Great Trees and then gone for help. Later, we would find her dead, murdered by the attackers who sought the Queen."

The Fanten hissed quietly through their teeth, expressing their sorrow and fury.

"Under the Great Trees, Queen Alinore struggled to give birth. Her labor pains had started as she fled up the slope of the ravine. Through the long day, as the battle cries of Shulen echoed through the forest, she gritted her teeth in silence. When I arrived, I went straight to the cave my daughter had shown me in the dream. Soldiers combed the woods. Shulen lay near death below. Queen Alinore showed the courage of all mothers, bringing her child into such a dangerous world. But she was weak and exhausted, already burning with the fever that would soon steal the breath from her body. She must have heard the black river of death roaring in her ears even as her child slipped through the waters of life into my hands. In the midst of all this violence drenching our woods in blood and danger, she made me promise to put the Mark of Peace on the child, the ancient symbol of a land united."

Fanten Grandmother's sharp gaze swept the silent and breathless crowd and fell on Ari Ara.

"The Queen begged me to hide the child and to protect her. How could I refuse? I swore on the honor of the Great Mother Tree and all my mothers before me: the child would be kept safe. The Queen lay back then and surrendered to the black river that pulled her out of this world."

The Fanten trilled in a soft keening, honoring a mother lost and a child born into such a dangerous world. Ari Ara's throat tightened. She blinked fiercely against the prickle in her eyes. Around the crowd, heads bowed and hands rose to wipe aside tears.

"For eleven years, we hid Ari Ara, though her blood made it difficult. She could not follow us into the deep Fanten sleep. Every winter I feared I would have to break my vow to Queen Alinore and turn her over to the lowlanders."

Fanten Grandmother smiled proudly.

"But, she proved strong as the Fanten, and when the sheep chose her as their shepherdess, we sent her into the High Mountains where no one but the spirits and legends dared to tread. This autumn, the girl took her fate into her own hands. She chose the Way Between, the path that would lead her to where she was meant to be!"

Her ringing tones evoked a burst of cheering and applause from the crowd. Ari Ara felt the heat of a blush climbing her neck. Under the commotion, Head Monk leaned over with a breathless rush of questions that the old woman steadily ignored.

Korin said in an undertone to the small group, "Friends, my head is pounding with as many questions as yours, but perhaps now is not the time for them. The Mark on her back confirms the story and I recommend," he suggested, "that we let the villagers celebrate. We can talk later in the privacy of Head Monk's office."

Head Monk looked mutinous. Fanten Grandmother smirked. Ari Ara doubted they'd get another word out of her. Shulen's expression revealed little, but he nodded his head in assent to Korin's suggestion. No one asked Ari Ara.

Korin called for wine and drinks. He waved at the fiddler to strike up a tune for dancing and set about shaking hands with everyone cheerfully, repeating to each person, "Astonishing, isn't it? The Lost Heir! Found at last!" Gradually the shock gave way to the thrill of excitement and much wine-laden celebration.

It was the strangest night of Ari Ara's life. The Fanten Grandmother, for once, did not abandon her side. Her presence had a quelling effect on the inquiries of others. Shulen, too, hovered at her elbow as if she might take off running. *Which,* she thought silently, *was very tempting.*

She stumbled through the motions with her heart pounding in her chest, her head burning with questions, and a sense that there had been a terrible mistake. She couldn't be the Lost Heir! Not her! Ari Ara of the High Mountains, *not this, not that,* constantly in trouble, illiterate until a few months ago. Her limbs wouldn't respond properly and she nearly knocked over Korin's wine glass twice. After the second time, she curled her fingers together in her lap and stared at the beautiful white silk of Queen Alinore's dress, stunned. Tentatively, she unfurled one finger and stroked the gold threads stitched in intricate patterns.

Shulen watched her, thinking of the terrible Fanten sense of irony that led the old woman to put the child back in the dress she had been wrapped in at birth. How well he knew that dress - the silk from Tahkan Shirar had been a wedding gift to Alinore. Rhianne, the Fanten Grandmother's daughter, had sewn it in the unique low-backed style of her people. She had been placing the final embroidery on the edges when they had fled. Shulen could see the section of the hem where the gold threads abruptly vanished.

Shulen sighed and crouched down beside Ari Ara where she sat dwarfed by the large chair of the village leader, looking stunned and half-terrified. She glanced at him with such confused anxiety that he put aside his inner turmoil and smiled gently at her.

"Cheer up, kitten," he said in a teasing tone. "You haven't sprouted horns. You just discovered you have royal parents,

230

that's all." He mock-glared at her. "Don't let it go to your head."

She gave him a weak smile. Shulen thought of Alinore. A memory he hadn't glimpsed in years slipped through his mind. He had been the Queen's guard since she was very young, and he recalled finding her as a child, curled in a ball of misery, upset to tears over the state of the world. Shulen eyed Ari Ara with the weary realization that she would be the third generation of Marianan queens under his watch. He felt old, as if it had been hundreds of years since he was chosen to be Alinore's guard and an eternity since being assigned to Elsinore when he was younger than Emir was now. He tapped the arm of the chair thoughtfully.

"We can't always tell what the day will bring, can we?" he said, half to himself, half to Ari Ara.

She shook her head.

"No," she agreed, thinking of all that had transpired since she tried to tell Shulen the dream that morning. Then she lifted her chin with a touch of her usual spirit and added, "but we can always rise to greet it, right Shulen?"

That's my girl, Shulen thought proudly. His heart lurched over the phrase. He nodded and stood swiftly, so she wouldn't read the shadows of thought crossing his face.

Korin buoyed them through the strangeness of it all with his easy geniality and smooth turns of phrases. The curly haired youth guided Ari Ara through the awkward moments with the air of one born to privilege and used to being obeyed unquestioningly. Around midnight, he leaned over to Ari Ara and whispered, "I always thought you'd be a boy . . . but any girl who can best Emir Miresh has a special place in my esteem."

She swiveled in her seat and flashed a rare grin. Korin blinked in surprise as her solemn face shone with sincere glee.

He regarded her steadily, impressed at the eleven year old who still sat straight-backed at midnight. She held herself with the pride and presence of the most regal Fanten Grandmothers.

For a moment, he saw the spirits of Queen Alinore and the Desert King threaded through the bones of her face. He blinked in awe. This redheaded girl was half-legend to him. As large as the Great Ones loomed in her life, so had his missing cousin hung over him. He leaned back in his seat, hiding his grin behind a yawn.

Welcome back, legend, he thought cheekily. After sixteen years of preparation and pressure, he was not wholly displeased at the thought of handing over the responsibilities he had been slated to bear. The blonde youth smiled in mischievous anticipation . . . he could hardly wait to introduce this wild creature to his overpowering mother. If she thought he was a hopeless case . . .

Korin began to laugh. Ari Ara cast a glance at him. Her lips twitched as if sensing some of the humor in the oddness of the night. And right there, with that burst of connection, he decided she would have his support through everything. *Ari Ara of the royal houses of Marin and Shirar*, he thought, testing the sound of her full name, *I hope the world is ready for you!*

CHAPTER TWENTY-SEVEN

. . . . .

The hour turned into the deep black of morning. The villagers had either gone to bed or were well into their cups, swapping outrageous stories about how they'd known all along that the redheaded shepherdess was the Lost Heir.

As for the girl, she had curled up in the village leader's large chair, rested her head on the arm, tucked her feet under the beautiful silk dress, and fallen asleep. For some time now, as Korin - with Miresh behind him like a shadow - flirted with a pair of wide-eyed and giggling girls on the other side of the village center, Shulen and the Fanten Grandmother had stood like a pair of sentinels, imposing and protective. They had not spoken, but as the night crept into the reverberating stillness of the early hours of a new day, the time arrived when old secrets are spilled and burning questions slip out like a sigh.

"I've wanted to speak with you since I arrived," Shulen said softly to the old woman.

She stared straight ahead as if fascinated by the configuration of stars shining over the Old Monk Mountain in the black pool of night.

"There is nothing to say, Shulen," she finally remarked.

"Yes, there is," he replied.

She waited.

"I'm sorry," the weathered grey man admitted, thinking of Rhianne, the Fanten Grandmother's daughter. "I loved her."

"If you truly loved her, then you should have quit your warrior ways and kept my daughter safe by giving up the sword, not bringing her into danger," Fanten Grandmother spat out, having waited eleven years and many long months to say those words to his face.

Shulen lowered his eyes.

"You're right," he agreed quietly.

A stunned surprise fell over the aloof woman. When she turned to see his bowed head, there was something more than anger in her eyes. It could not quite be called compassion . . . but perhaps a small gleam of understanding hinted in her gaze. She drew breath to say, in all fairness, that she knew the depth of love that had existed between her daughter and the warrior, but Shulen spoke first and the Fanten Grandmother retreated into the comfort of her silence.

"I was sworn to the Guard when I was younger than Emir Miresh," Shulen told her. "I was raised to it from childhood. I have spent my life protecting the queens of Mariana. Only three times in over four decades of service have I considered walking away from it all."

Fanten Grandmother listened with the air of one who does not like the words, but is willing to hear them out.

"The first," Shulen confessed, "was the day I met your daughter Rhianne. For forty years, I had lived and breathed my loyalty to the queens, but when I met Rhianne, I went straight to Alinore and tried to resign. My loyalties would be forever split, I warned her. But Alinore just laughed and decided to befriend Rhianne, bringing her into her close circle . . . you know how she was, always connecting impossible alliances."

Fanten Grandmother nodded. She remembered. A bittersweet memory of the young woman rose in her mind. She had spent many years regretting the tragic end of the deep friendship that grew between the Queen and her daughter. Alinore had a magic to her ways; she made love between enemies possible.

Shulen spoke again.

"The second time I wanted to quit was the day our daughter was born. I held her - so fragile, so small - and the thought struck me that all of my life prior to that moment had been a long tragedy, a worthless waste. Swords and battles mattered less than dried cow dung in a fallow field. This beauty of a child was the only worthwhile thing I had ever contributed to the world. Every day in service of the Great Ones, every day following the ways of *Attar* was an affront to the beauty of the child I held. Had I known what little time remained to my family, and that my daughter would die on the same day as her mother, I would have broken my sword over my knee and left the warrior's path forever."

This was new knowledge to the Fanten Grandmother, and her heart stirred uneasily. Her eyes flicked to the Stone One and thought, perhaps, she had misjudged him. For the first time in many years, she felt the painful flutter of nervousness in her chest.

Shulen continued speaking in a low rumble of a tone that only she could hear.

"But war is a lie with a silver-lined tongue. It convinces you that only by the sword can you protect the ones you love. So, I stuck by my sword . . . and they died because of that choice."

This time, the silence stretched long between his next words. His eyes were lost in shadows and darkness. The Fanten Grandmother stood as still as the Stone One. Had she known the cold warrior could love so deeply . . . care so tenderly . . . had she known how close he stood to renouncing *Attar* . . . had she known how the smallest word from her might have changed the course of events . . . she had spoken cruelly to him in those terrible times, especially when he lay near death in the forest after the battle of Shulen's Stand. The sight of her daughter's murdered body had driven her mad with grief. Wracked with a terrible hatred of the man who had led her daughter into danger, she had made certain choices . . . she shuddered. It had seemed to her, in those days, that the daughter of Shulen was a vile creature, tainted with the blood of her father. She had not regretted telling him of her loss.

But now, years later, the Stone One was a man burdened by grief, no longer a statue of a warrior, but a human, one who had once, all too briefly, been a father.

"The third time I wanted to quit the Guard and renounce *Attar*," Shulen said, interrupting her thoughts, "was on the day I arrived at Monk's Hand Monastery to train the warriors and a girl dodged a dozen monks, determined to pursue her own path through life."

He smiled at Ari Ara with such affection that Fanten Grandmother felt the mist of tears rising in her eyes. Aghast at herself, she blinked them back firmly.

"You are one of the few people who will remember," Shulen mused thoughtfully, looking at the red-haired girl, "that in my youth, my hair was brighter than the Desert King's, as was my father's, and his father's, and," his voice turned hard-edged, "my daughter's whom you told me you buried in the Fanten woods."

Fanten Grandmother swallowed her memories and steeled herself for his next words.

"So, you are also the only living person who can imagine what I felt, seeing a girl with flame-colored hair, dancing the Fanten dances like Rhianne, taking to *Azar* as if . . . she . . . had . . . been . . . born for it."

Shulen twisted his words like knife wounds into the old woman's gut. She lifted her eyes in alarm and saw the burning intensity of his emotions. His muscles tensed with a fury that had no name.

"I have always known you were cruel," Shulen spat at her, "and so, for many months, I suspected that you might, indeed, be vicious enough to hide my daughter from me . . . but tonight I learned that your hatred of me knows no bounds. For you allowed me to believe - for one brief season - that one of the secret longings of my heart was true, that my daughter was still alive, only to snatch that joy from me tonight."

Fanten Grandmother drew on every fiber of her strength to keep from flinching.

"Was that your revenge, then?" he growled at her. "To let me spend this time with this child, believing that by some miracle my daughter had lived, and grown, and had not died on that hated day along with her mother . . . only to reveal her as Alinore and Tahkan's child?"

Shulen straightened and faced the old woman.

"Hear this, Lianne," he said, using her given name and stripping from her the stature of her rank and title. "I swear by my love of Rhianne which remains undiminished to this day, that your cruelty has failed . . . for no matter whose bloodlines gave rise to this child, no matter whose womb carried her, no matter whose seed started her . . . Ari Ara is the daughter of my heart, and that is something nothing - not you, not the thrones, not the Desert King, not time, not even death - will take away."

And though the Stone One's voice had not risen from a low murmur, Fanten Grandmother felt his words thundering in her ears. Her body felt as if it had turned to stone and piece-by-piece was crumbling into dust. A thousand words brimmed in her throat, but she could not open her mouth to speak. The man who had led her daughter to her death stood undiminished, unbroken, made whole by the strength of love that defied bloodlines and lineages and all expectations. He would guard over not a third generation of Marianan queens, but rather a child whom he cared for in her own right.

"Get out of my sight," Shulen growled at the Fanten woman. "I never want to see you again."

The Fanten Grandmother spun and fled into the silence and darkness of her ways. She had one last secret clutched in her chest . . . and she vowed furiously that she would carry it to her grave. Her mocking laughter ran out, but Shulen did not hear it as he lifted the sleeping girl and began the long walk up the stone steps of the monastery.

CHAPTER TWENTY-EIGHT

. . . . .

Clang. Clang. Clang. Ari Ara bolted awake at the sound of the temple bell's raucous ringing. For a brief moment, she thought it had all been a long, strange dream. She was back in her closet, wearing her old training clothes, tucked under the shepherdess cloak. The dress was gone.

A sudden thought struck her. Her fingers flew to the top of her head where her curls worked loose from the unmistakable pattern of the Fanten braids. The knotted blue tie the women had used slipped free. She held it in her hand as the events of the night before flooded back. She remembered waking briefly, being carried by someone - Shulen - up the long steps as the sigh of night hung thick around them. She had been sleepily glad of the quiet, the darkness, the stars shimmering in the black sky, the coolness of the spring air. The soft voices and footsteps of others sounded like water lapping the edges of river rocks, gentle and lulling. In the night, she sensed the subtle presence of the ancestor spirits lining the stairs. At the landing, she saw the Fanten woman from the woods - the daughter of the Fanten Grandmother - and it seemed like the spirit was trying to speak. Shulen could not hear her and simply continued climbing the stairs.

At the top landing, she heard low-voiced discussions whispering all around. Shulen spoke once or twice, his voice a deep rumble of sound. Then he walked toward the senior monks' corridor. Her limbs felt like deadwood. Every bit of her body ached with exhaustion, and when she finally exchanged the beautiful dress for her spare training clothes and crawled into her cubbyhole over the objections of the Head Monk (the Lost Heir couldn't sleep in a closet!), her muddled thoughts murmured in half-sentences and unfinished questions. She tossed and turned and thought she would never fall asleep, but she must have because she woke up at the sound of the temple bell.

Ari Ara sighed, rubbed her fingers vigorously over her scalp to wake up, and shook the tangles out of her hair. Then she slid open the door and rolled out.

"Oomph!" she exclaimed as she landed on something.

Miresh was sitting beside her door.

"What are you doing?" she asked stupidly, feeling as groggy as he looked.

"Guarding you."

"From what? Rock beetles?" she asked in an incredulous tone.

"Shhh," he hissed. "Don't wake everyone up."

Ari Ara groaned and stood up. Miresh began to rise.

"I'm just going to get some water," she grumbled. "Nowhere else."

He looked skeptical.

"I'm done running," she stated with more conviction than she actually felt. She turned on her heel and was gratified when he did not follow.

Ari Ara poured a cup of fresh water from the jar near the kitchen and was surprised to see the sun so high in the sky. No one seemed to be up and about except for the orphans - who were probably the ones ringing the temple bell out of sheer mischief and boredom. The group that had been playing a game on the training sands ran over when they saw her. They crowded around, jostling and whispering, pointing at her back. Awed and curious expressions shone in each face. One older orphan wouldn't meet her eye.

"So, is it true?" a small boy asked.

Ari Ara nodded.

"They say there's a Mark on my back to prove it," she said.

"Can we see it?" he asked daringly.

She nodded again and they pressed closer, pulling down the back of her tunic so hard she nearly choked. She imagined the messenger hawk to the Capital: *Lost Heir found, but accidently strangled by over-enthusiastic orphans.* The shorter children complained that they couldn't see, so she knelt in the center of the huddled youths as they touched the Mark in a strange mixture of delight and daring. The orphans blurted out all the questions that had churned in her since the dance in the village.

"Do you remember her? Queen Alinore?"

"Will you go to the Capital?"

"When do you meet the Desert King?"

She stood up and shooed the orphans back.

"So," commented a soft voice behind her, "the Lost Heir has awakened."

Minli stood behind her, leaning on his crutch, his eyes crinkled at the corners. The orphans ran off, giggling behind their hands and whispering.

"Pinch me, Minli," she suggested. "Hard. I think I'm stuck in a strange dream."

He obliged. She winced. Definitely not dreaming, she decided.

"Check the Mark . . . and tell me if it's really there," she said, turning around.

He glanced down the back of her tunic.

"Yup. It's there, burned into your skin, stained black with ink."

"Does it look like - "

"Just like the mark on the Third Brother's book."

"We were right!" she exclaimed, wide-eyed. She turned back around in time to see him laughing.

"Only about that!" Minli pointed out.

"Thank the ancestors you taught me how to read," Ari Ara exclaimed. "Korin and everyone just about died of shock knowing I tended Fanten sheep in the High Mountains. Good thing I didn't tell them I couldn't read or write until a few months ago."

Minli spluttered with laughter.

"Or that Shulen threw you in the river! "

"Or the time he made me scrub all those eggs off the steps!"

"Or stand on top of the ancestor pillar all day."

They laughed.

"I'm still me, Minli," she said quietly.

He nodded somberly, then shrugged and grinned.

"It's just hard to imagine *you* being the Lost Heir."

"I still think you should have been the Lost Heir," she grumbled. "You probably know the proper way to greet a royal aunt."

"We don't get to choose our fates," Minli sighed, looking at his missing leg.

"Rubbish," Ari Ara retorted. "I don't believe that."

Minli raised an eyebrow.

"Brave words for someone who has the Mark of the Lost Heir on her back . . . and the Prophecy hanging over her head."

She had forgotten about the Prophecy. She was about to say more when the temple bell started clanging again. Head Monk emerged from his quarters looking decidedly disgruntled.

"Stop that racket immediately!" he bellowed.

Second Monk stumbled out rubbing his eyes and was sent to go apprehend the culprits, but the noise had succeeded in rousing the monastery. Monks and trainees poured out half-awake and disheveled. They appeared as rattled as Ari Ara felt. They bowed as they passed her, some gracefully, others in a strange jerk of motion as if they couldn't quite believe that she was the Lost Heir. A confused flurry of questions filled the courtyard until Head Monk took charge. He sent the youngest orphans with Scholar Monk, set the trainees to chores, and stared at Ari Ara as if he didn't quite know what to do with her.

"Ahem, yes, well, your highness," Head Monk began, tripping over his own tongue.

Ari Ara fought the urge to laugh - or cry. Minli snorted with humor.

"You'd best get used to it," Korin suggested in a cheerful voice hoarse with lack of sleep. "There are far worse titles: your supreme royalness, your most magnanimous. My favorite was being called your most pretentiousness, though I doubt the poor girl knew what she meant . . . at least, I hope not."

Korin nodded sagely at Minli.

"You'll want a few good friends who will call you a hard-nosed dunderhead when you're about to do something particularly idiotic." He winked at the one-legged boy. "Think you can handle that?"

Minli grinned at Ari Ara. Relief flooded through her limbs. Minli wouldn't treat her like she walked on clouds and farted roses. She could rely on him for honesty.

"Now, where might I get a strong cup of tea?" Korin asked. "My head is throbbing like someone has been hammering a great bell all morning."

"They were," Emir Miresh answered, walking toward them while hauling a pair of orphans along by the collars.

"We just thought the whole world ought to know the Lost Heir's been found!" one boy said defensively.

"Yeah, we were ringing it for her," his companion added.

"And because we always wanted to do that," the first muttered under his breath.

Head Monk fought to hide his smile.

"Off you go. No punishments today in honor of the discovery of the heir, but you're to go straight to Scholar Monk and ask about the proper way to announce auspicious tidings when ringing a sacred temple bell!"

The boys groaned and ran toward the Teaching Room. Teapot Monk emerged, rubbing his head and waving at the group.

"Hot tea in a few minutes," he mumbled.

Ari Ara suspected he'd go straight for the hangover remedy he kept on the top shelf of the tinctures.

Shulen appeared. He looked as if he hadn't slept a moment, but when his eyes met Ari Ara's across the training sands, the haggard shadows in his face lifted. He crossed over to the group.

"Tea?" he asked.

"In my office," Head Monk invited, gesturing.

Ari Ara was motioned to join them. She glanced at Minli and Head Monk caught the exchange.

"Minli, you come take notes. We'll need a good hand for messages, I expect," Head Monk ordered. Minli looked delighted at the suggestion. Korin gestured for the two young ones to enter then followed them into Head Monk's office. Shulen pulled up a stool next to Ari Ara. Miresh stood by the door, watching everything and missing nothing.

Teapot Monk brought hot water, cups, and strong tea then departed to take command of the kitchen. Shulen poured for everyone, quiet and pensive, watching the water flow from spout to cup with the studied attention of one determined to keep his thoughts steady. Korin waited for all to be served, then lifted his cup in a gesture of honor to Ari Ara, who squirmed uncomfortably and hoped no one expected a speech. The others joined their cups to Korin's, though Minli appeared to be on the verge of laughing and Miresh winked at her, which made the seriousness of Head Monk and Shulen bearable.

"So, where shall we begin?" Head Monk asked at last.

"I sent a messenger hawk to my mother last night," Korin answered. "Her reply will undoubtedly be swift. Once it arrives, we'll have to inform several others, including the Desert King, perhaps."

"Perhaps?" Ari Ara blurted out.

"Well, these are matters of state," Korin stammered, a bit flustered.

"It has already been done," Shulen said in a firm voice.

Korin swiveled to frown at the older man.

"By whom? On whose orders?"

"By me, and on order of my conscience," Shulen answered calmly.

"The Great Lady is not going to be happy with you, Shulen," Korin stated.

"I have known Brinelle for many years," the old warrior sighed. "She is often not happy with me - or anyone - and she hasn't managed to hang me yet."

Ari Ara spun to him in alarm.

"They'll hang you for telling the Desert King?"

"No," Korin assured her with a disgusted snort. "He's a national hero. We can't get rid of him no matter how much we want to."

He sounded so annoyed that Ari Ara suspected it was true. She studied her royal cousin and decided there was more under that curly head of hair than charm.

"Why wouldn't the Desert King be told right away?" she asked.

Korin and Head Monk exchanged glances.

"It's complicated," Korin began to say.

"No, it's not," Shulen answered quietly, his eyes fixed on the youth. "The Marianan nobles stand at an advantage if they hold the Heir to the Desert . . . and an even greater advantage if they know it and Tahkan doesn't."

"Oh come, Shulen," Korin said crossly. "We're at war, or close enough to it."

"You're not at war," Ari Ara stated firmly. "Not any more. The nobles can't invade the desert to find me if I'm sitting under their noses, can they?"

Miresh and Shulen exchanged a look.

"What?" Ari Ara asked. "You mean, they would?"

"They might," Shulen confirmed. "Or they'd provoke the Desert People into invading Mariana."

The old warrior tapped his finger on the table.

"That's one reason I sent a message to the Desert King, hoping to avert hostilities with an act of good faith." Shulen's eyes darkened. "I am not certain he will accept it, especially coming from me, but I have reason to hope that he might."

In the sleepless night, he had written a dozen drafts of the message to Tahkan Shirar, and burned all but the last. In this, he called upon the days of their friendship and mutual respect, and - in an act of near treason - apologized for his role in the War of Retribution. He told Tahkan his daughter had been found, that she had his hair and her mother's eyes, and begged the king to hold steady through the madness of the nobles' machinations. He promised to bring her to the desert as soon as possible. He had closed with a final word upon which his hopes hung. *As a father who also lost his wife and daughter on that day,* he wrote, *you have my word that I will lay down my life before any harm comes to your child.*

All he could do was wait.

"A father who has lost his daughter has a right to know that she has been found," Shulen said simply to the others. He shut his eyes for a moment then continued. "This, too, must be addressed: we allowed our nobles to launch the War of Retribution based on the lie that desert factions had killed Queen Alinore. But, the truth is that the bodies of those I killed in the ravine were from the borders and were mostly likely mercenaries who were loyal only to the purse that paid them. The only thing I know with certainty is that Tahkan Shirar would never have killed the woman that he loved."

Shulen stopped, frowning at his hands.

"War is always madness, but this one more so than most. Such bloodshed over nothing. I am as much to blame as any. My sword was thirsty for revenge, and I wanted to believe the nobles' lies when they claimed they had proof of the identity of the attackers. But when I think of Tahkan Shirar . . . a man whom I knew and respected . . . when I think of his despair, having lost his love, his child, and then so many of his people to our invading armies over half-truths and uncertainties . . . "

Shulen broke off, shaking his head.

"Someone must make right the wrongs, impossible as the task may be," he said, turning to Korin. "Mariana must apologize to the Desert King and his people, and beg forgiveness for what we did."

"Come now, Shulen," Head Monk replied indignantly, "We did not know - "

"Is that any excuse?" Shulen cried. "Who will apologize?"

"I will."

Ari Ara startled everyone by speaking. They turned to stare at her.

"I'll apologize. I grew up as an orphan of both sides. I'll apologize for us all."

She sat upright in her chair with as much dignity as she could muster.

"But that should only be the start," she added, glancing at Minli, "because the people on both sides have suffered and caused harm in equal measures. In the Third Brother's book, we read about processes that can help us speak painful truths, listen deeply to one another, and begin to heal."

She saw a flash of understanding leap across Shulen and Miresh's faces. They, too, had read the stories.

"We can do as Alaren did with the bandits," she said firmly, "and start to deal with the hurt and harm."

She has thought about this for some time, Shulen realized. The one-legged boy was nodding along in a way that suggested long hours of dreaming and discussion had transpired while the rest of the monastery was busy training for war.

Ari Ara smiled gently and winningly at each person in a manner that reminded Shulen of Alinore trying to convince people to one of her improbable causes. He drew breath to comment on it, but Korin beat him to the words.

"By the ancestors, she looks like Aunt Alinore," Korin breathed in awe. His memories were hazy, but the Queen's portrait hung in the Capital, and the eyes of the mother blazed in the daughter.

Shulen silently agreed, thinking it appropriate that Alinore, the peacemaker, had joined the worlds of Mariana and the Desert, water and fire, into this child. He sent a prayer to her spirit to tell her that her greatest gift to her people was sitting among them, alive. He thought of the thousands of unlikely alliances Alinore had forged and the love she had sparked in so many hearts. For over a decade, all that had appeared lost, but with the discovery of the heir, they had found far more than a child. They will look at Ari Ara, Shulen knew, and they will remember her mother. When they see her eyes, those long-buried seeds and forgotten bonds of friendships will burst through the darkness of these years. There will be harms to mend and wounds to heal - Shulen's eyes widened as the words of the prophecy rang through his mind.

By the Mark of Peace, the lost one is found. Then the once broken becomes whole, the once wounded healed, and the once forgotten remembered again.

Shulen shifted in his seat. His eyes gleamed. He shivered as he remembered something forgotten.

"Ari Ara," he said, "you told me you had a dream."

The others broke off their conversation in curiosity at his words.

"Yes," she said, her voice a bare murmur as she glanced up in surprise.

"In the dream, you swam up the black river of ancestors and met the Three Brothers. Alaren gave you a message."

249

"You *were* listening," she sighed.

"Yes, though not as well as I should have been," Shulen conceded with a soft smile of apology. "I was distracted by war and worry, but I wanted to tell you . . . the thing you asked of me . . . my answer has changed."

The two stared at each other. The others frowned in confusion. The lines in the corners of Shulen's eyes curved upwards. Ari Ara's hands flew to her mouth in shocked delight.

"Really? You will? I mean, *can you?*"

Shulen's wry smile answered.

"I imagine so. I am, after all, the Head of the Guard, Great Warrior, and the master of the two most legendary apprentices in Marianan history."

"What on earth are you two grinning about?" interrupted Korin.

"Bringing back *Azar*," the pair said on the same breath.

"To the warriors," Ari Ara explained.

"To the Guard," Shulen added.

"To the nobles," she reminded him.

"To everyone," he agreed.

A stunned silence fell.

"They'll never go along with it," Head Monk stated.

"Yes, they will," Emir Miresh replied quietly in a confident tone. "Especially when the Champion supports it."

Shulen met Miresh's eyes across the table. Then he held out his hand, palm up, in the handshake of one warrior honoring another. Emir's eyes glowed and a deep blush climbed the curves of his cheekbones as he stretched out his hand to his teacher. The two joined hands in the symbol of enduring loyalty and commitment.

"Thank you," Shulen said to Emir.

"I had to," the youth replied with an easy smile. "She bested me in that unsanctioned Trial . . . I want a rematch in the Capital or a chance to train up someone who will thoroughly trounce her."

He grinned at Ari Ara to let her know he was joking.

"You'll beat me next time," she said graciously. "And Shulen always wins."

"Not for long," the old warrior murmured. "There will be many who join the first three followers of *Azar*."

A hand shot out across the table to join the warriors' handshake.

"Four," Minli said with quiet dignity and nervousness. His face flushed from neck to brow at his own daring. "I may not be fast on my feet - or foot, as it is - but I'm a follower of *Azar*, too."

His eyes turned moist and Ari Ara saved him from his anxiousness at joining hands with the two most powerful warriors in all of Mariana by sliding her hand on top of his in the center of the table.

"You can run circles around me in inner *Azar* any day," she praised him.

Shulen, who knew more of the children's secrets than they suspected, said to the boy, "You honor us by being a follower of Alaren's Way Between."

Minli turned a shade of scarlet to match his friend's hair, but she could tell by the trembling of his hand under hers that this moment meant more to the one-legged orphan than he could ever express in words.

A fifth hand joined theirs: Korin's.

"I'll throw my lot in with you," he told them, "if only to see the look on Mother's face when we tell her the days of warring are done."

He grinned with rebellious anticipation.

Shulen cleared his throat to remind the youth that *Azar* was not about taking a jab at one's mother - but Head Monk's hand reached out and joined the clasp of solidarity.

"And I swear this monastery to your course," he said with passion.

They turned to him in surprise.

Head Monk's face took on an expression of dignity and strength.

"This is where Ari Ara is from. She was born over the ridge, raised in the Fanten Forest and in the High Mountains, trained in *Azar* at our monastery, and discovered to be the Lost Heir in the village below."

He straightened his spine with pride.

"It's only fitting that we should follow her in the way of *Azar*. All of us at Monk's Hand Monastery, from the smallest orphan to the oldest monk, will devote ourselves to learning her way."

Ari Ara was about to protest that it was Alaren's way, not hers, when Shulen shook his head imperceptibly. She allowed the Head Monk the dignity of the moment, and thus learned her first lesson in statesmanship, diplomacy, and tact.

Shulen looked around the small circle bound by the clasp of friendship, purpose, and vision. This was only the beginning, he thought, and he found his old heart already rising to the adventure ahead.

CHAPTER TWENTY-NINE

. . . . .

That night, after hours of meetings and endless cups of tea, Ari Ara snagged Shulen by the elbow as they all surrendered to the need for sleep.

"Shulen . . . can we talk?"

She had questions burning holes in her heart and the yearning for answers jangled her nerves wide awake.

"Let's go sit on the landing," he suggested quietly.

The night's fresh air was a relief after the long day inside the crowded office. The rest of the monastery had retired and the only sounds were giggles from the orphans' wing and Second Monk's scolding. Shulen sank onto the firm smoothness of the stone steps. Ari Ara sat down in a ball, pulling her knees to her chest and wrapping her arms around them.

"What do you want to talk about?" he asked.

"Everything," she sighed wistfully, knowing that the whole night would not be long enough to answer all of her questions. "But first, I wanted to thank you."

The words sounded odd in her throat, as if jumbled up with dozens of other things she wanted to say to him as well.

"Thank you for standing up for *Azar*," she added, "and for teaching me, and . . . and for everything."

She swallowed.

"And thank you for sending the message to the Desert King."

"A father has a right to know where his daughter is," Shulen replied, echoing his earlier words. "I would want to know."

Silence fell for a moment.

"Shulen?" Ari Ara asked nervously. "What's he like?"

"Tahkan Shirar?" the older man guessed at her thought. "He is a remarkable person."

He grinned in the darkness.

"You will like him," he told the girl, who reminded him strongly of the headstrong Desert King. "He is proud to a fault, stubborn beyond reason, and courageous. Tahkan is a passionate person. Like his desert, he can be both harsh and breathlessly stunning. He is a man of integrity and intensity. I was honored to once call him my friend."

"Once?"

"I waged war on his people, Ari Ara. I failed to protect his wife."

She thought for a long moment.

"Perhaps, someday, he'll find a way to forgive you, and you can both repair the friendship you lost."

"You sound like your mother," Shulen said without thinking.

"I do?" Ari Ara replied in a flutter of nervous surprise. "Tell me about her . . . please?"

Her heart thudded in her chest as she waited for him to respond.

"She was many things," Shulen said, "beautiful, royal, proud. I remember her at your age. You could not be less alike."

Ari Ara's expression fell. She bit back her disappointment.

Shulen smiled gently as if sensing her reaction.

"She was pampered, over-indulged, and imperious. None of which describes you."

Ari Ara smiled tentatively back. She couldn't argue with that.

"Queen Alinore grew into a strong young woman who took her responsibilities very seriously. Her one act of rebellion was to love the Desert King."

Shulen shook his head, remembering.

"Had it not ended so tragically, their story would be the source of the greatest love ballads of our time."

"So, he did love her?" Ari Ara asked breathlessly.

"As deeply as she loved him," Shulen confirmed. "No matter what anyone tells you, Ari Ara, never doubt it. I was there. I know the truth of what they felt for one another. You are the creation of a great love, the likes of which we rarely see."

Ari Ara hugged her knees to her chest, hardly able to breath.

"Shulen?" she whispered with a tremor in her voice. "Do you think . . . if she were still alive, do you think she would have liked me?"

The Stone One's chiseled expression softened. His grey eyes grew moist. He reached out an arm and hugged her shoulders.

"Ari Ara," he answered, "she would have loved you more than you can ever imagine."

CHAPTER THIRTY

. . . . .

The day of departure came swift as the winds howling over
the peaks of the Monk's Hand Mountains. The stairs were
lined with trainees, orphans, monks, and villagers. The lines
stretched all the way to the Thumb's Pass. Three times the
Horns of Monk's Hand thundered. The mountains roared with
echoes. As the rolling reverberations faded, the throb of the
Fanten drums rose in the distance.

Ari Ara knew the song. It was a farewell to those who were
going, wishing them safe journeys until they returned. To the
Fanten, endings were always beginnings, one season turned over
into the next, one body gave birth to another, and the story
always went on. There were no goodbyes among the Fanten,
only momentary farewells until meeting again.

The messenger hawks had returned from the Capital and
from the Desert. The Great Lady ordered them to come at
once. The Desert King sent formal state greetings to his heir -
and a private note to Shulen.

For those mortals who cannot fly like spirits or hawks or the
excitement of our racing hearts, the journey to the Desert takes many
weeks of travel, and there are further obstacles of politics to cross . . .

257

but I will be ready when you send word. You honor me with your message, Stone One.

He signed it in the old way, as he had in the days before Alinore's death. And to Ari Ara he sent a gift: a black-winged falcon named Shadow, a blank stack of messenger scrolls, and a short note.

Write to me, daughter, for the years have been long. I wish to know of your life, and in this small way, start to make up for all that has been lost. The bird will come only to me . . . and if you win his trust, then he will seek you out through the worst of storms to carry our messages to each other.

She had sent a reply right away, although it was difficult to find the words, and she was ashamed of the awkwardness of her brushstrokes. Minli offered to write out her message, but she felt it was something she had to do on her own. She had watched the falcon soar west from Monk's Hand with a wildly beating heart. When the stretch of the bird's black wings vanished from sight, she sensed the closing of one chapter of her life . . . and the opening of another looming before her.

Today, Ari Ara gazed at the crater of the valley. Her heart throbbed and ached at the same time. Every beautiful line of Monk's Hand etched in her vision. The squat thatched houses of the villagers. The green fields and lower meadows dotted with white flocks. The dark crests of the Fanten Forest and the clear, cold water of the Monk's Tears River. Her gaze lifted to the High Mountains, the steep slopes and sweeping mists. The Old Monk Mountain watched over the stone-carved monastery tucked into his side.

Ari Ara smiled.

Monk's Hand Monastery would never be the same, though the stone walls seemed as ancient as ever. A contingent of warrior monks traveled with them to Mariana Capital . . . where they would study *Azar* with Shulen when he began to train everyone in the Way Between. Alaren's way was returning as surely as the grasses emerged after a long, cold winter. The archivist had set the best scribes to copying the Third Brother's book. Already, Scholar Monk was teaching the orphans lessons from its pages. This year, the monastery would be quieter and more studious than usual . . . but by next spring, the courtyard would ring with shouts of *Azar!*

On the heels of the announcement that Monk's Hand Monastery was dedicating its efforts to *Azar*, messenger hawks from the Capital stunned the monks - the major patrons of the monastery threatened to cut funding. They weren't going to feed a bunch of lily-livered cowards, one note said bluntly. Get back to *Attar* or starve. While Korin and Head Monk sent furious messages in reply, it was Teapot Monk who entered the fray with all the discipline, determination, and dedication of a Great Warrior.

Heaving his round belly down the long steps to the village, he struck a deal with the leader: the monks would help teach the children in exchange for a plot of land and a portion of the harvest of the village.

"You grow grain to sell to the nobles, who use it to feed warriors, who make wars to enrich the nobles, who then send us the money to train them more warriors," Teapot Monk explained to the village leader in a dizzying circle of connections. "This is madness. I want to grow grain, feed children, and raise followers of *Azar*. Help me do it."

The village leader clasped hands with the kitchen monk. Ari Ara cheered when she heard the news.

Ari Ara swept her eyes across all the familiar faces assembled at the gateway of the monastery. Though the warrior monks traveled with them, there were many who would stay behind. Among them was a small one-legged boy with a bird's nest of brown hair.

"It won't be forever," she told Minli, crossing over to him. "Scholar Monk promised you could come to the Capital."

"So long as I pass my summer exams," he added.

"Study hard then," she ordered. "I expect to see you by autumn . . . with the new curriculum in hand."

They swapped a grin. Minli had been tasked to work with Scholar Monk on drafting a curriculum on the Third Brother's book and the Way Between. They would test each lesson on the orphans, and Minli would bring it to the Capital when he came.

They flung their arms around each other.

"I'm on your heels," he promised.

She made the ritual rounds to all of the senior monks. Nobstick and Teapot Monk handed her a small gift.

"It's bread," Nobstick told her. "We remember how it used to amaze you."

She smiled, thinking back to her arrival at Monk's Hand Monastery.

"Don't lose that spirit," Teapot Monk urged her. "No matter how much they try to spoil you in the Capital, remember to always be grateful for a simple loaf of good bread."

She hugged them around their waists, startling the kitchen monks into smiles.

One by one, she bid farewell to the other monks, orphans, and trainees. She and Brol regarded each other with unsmiling expressions for a moment. Then she turned away without another word. Ari Ara felt Brol's stare drilling into her back and shivered imperceptibly. She wished she had found a way to make things right with him . . . but there was nothing she could do now. She set her chin and moved on.

The Fanten Grandmother was next. She and several of the other women had come down out of the forest to watch the girl depart. She stood on the far side of the landing, carefully avoiding Shulen. Their animosity seethed as hot as ever, but she had a right to be here, and the girl expected her presence. Not even the Stone One could stop her from coming to say farewell.

The Fanten Grandmother lifted her head defiantly. Her reasons were not as they seemed. Her story differed from his version. She had, after all, named and raised the girl, kept her alive, and nurtured her to greater strength than any could have imagined.

She turned to Ari Ara with honest affection. She held the child's face in her wrinkled hands, kissed her forehead as she did all the daughters, then said,

"Remember us and be our voice in the places where we have been forgotten."

Ari Ara nodded and promised she would. A chorus of Fanten women trilled.

Shulen stood by the gates, waiting as patiently as the stones of the mountains. He watched the girl proudly. She stood lightly on her feet, head held high. The black cloak he had given her rested on her shoulders. Her bright hair blazed against the hard blue of the sky. He smiled at the emotions shining her eyes, a mixture of sorrow and excitement dancing, letting go and leaping into the day.

Shulen turned to her and said something softly. Before she could reply, he gave her a little push toward the stairs.

The Horns sounded. She stepped out of the monastery. The temple bell rang.

And in that instant, the meaning of Shulen's words struck her as the Fanten women's trills rose.

"Let's go, daughter of my heart," he had said, "let's go and find the Way Between!"

The roar broke loose from her throat and leapt like a challenge to the world that waited.

"*Azar!*"

The End.

The Way Between

AUTHOR'S NOTE

. . . . .

Everybody loves a good story. Action, adventure, mystery, magic, great characters, moments of courage, heroics, heart . . . human beings delight in stories. Since time immemorial, we've been spinning legends, myths, epics, and sagas to inspire and educate our communities.

After four thousand years of war, violence, and conquest, it's time for some new stories. Our literature needs a 21st century update. If we look around the world today, the most exciting adventures of our times are unfolding in nonviolent movements for change. Here's just a few of the hundreds of stories: Gandhi liberating India from British Rule; the American Civil Rights Movement; Leymah Gbowee and the Liberian Mass Action for Peace ending the Second Liberian Civil War; Estonia's Singing Revolution, and the 50 nonviolent revolutions that have happened in the last 30 years.

New research shows that nonviolent action is on the rise . . . and violence is on the decline. And, nonviolent struggle is proving to be *twice* as effective as violence in achieving the very socio-political goals so often depicted in our epic literature: stopping invasions, overthrowing tyrants, and liberating the people. So, it's time to stop making our children read King

265

Arthur and Robin Hood, Hercules and Odysseus, and to start writing new stories that reflect the reality of our world today.

The Way Between is a story for our times. It offers the younger generations - and the older ones - the values of peace and nonviolence, anti-bullying, compassion, inclusion, and belonging. It challenges war, violence, discrimination, and prejudice. The story has all the beauty of the great stories of old: adventure, action, challenges, courage, secrets, and mysteries, surprises, friendship, and connection; but without the outdated glorification of war and violence.

In our modern world, we need stories, heroes and heroines, myths and legends, that offer the viable, amazing skills of peacebuilding, unarmed peacekeeping, restorative justice, conflict resolution, nonviolence and nonviolent action. Around the world, there are hundreds and thousands of stories of real people making change and confronting injustice through these skills. Our literature must rise to the times. Every schoolchild should be dreaming about civil disobedience instead of sword fighting; boycotts instead of bombs.

As an author, my pen is bent to this task, flying across the page to rewrite the cultural mythologies in our literature. If our children and our populace are to be trained for the world that is emerging, then we must put the tools of peace and active nonviolence in their hands, hearts, minds, dreams, and stories, today.

Toward a culture of peace and active nonviolence,

Rivera Sun

ACKNOWLEDGMENTS

. . . . .

A story comes into existence through the efforts of a whole web of people. I'd like to share a few words of gratitude for the countless actions, influences, and inspirations that supported this novel.

First, let me offer a deep bow of respect to the peace movement, which has spent decades exploring the profound possibilities of human beings to resolve conflict nonviolently. Despite great challenges, the many advocates of peace have persevered in developing phenomenal tactics for those instances when human beings disagree in large and small ways. This work is mythic, profound, and vitally important.

I wish to thank the Veterans for Peace, Nonviolent Peaceforce, Fellowship of Reconciliation, Code Pink, Shanti Sena Network, Metta Center for Nonviolence, Pace e Bene/Campaign Nonviolence, and many more organizations whose work has inspired many scenes in this book, not to mention saved lives and shifted cultures toward peace and active nonviolence.

Larsen Prip and David Soumis, I would like to thank you for your enduring inspiration. Your constant efforts as members of Veterans for Peace motivated me to do my part as a novelist toward our shared goals. Paul K. Chappell's writings on waging peace were very helpful. Sherri Mitchell, our friendship and conversations deepen and inform all of my writing work. David Hartsough, your life and writings have also been an inspiration. Michael Nagler and Stephanie Van Hook, you will see your influence in many pages of this book. Maja Bengtson, our Swedish-American conversations have lent many insights into the importance of culture and belief. Kathy Kelly, thank you for reminding me of the importance of storytelling in the work that we do. Medea Benjamin and Jodie Evans, thank you for the Peace Economy without which Teapot Monk would not have taken his bold actions at the end. Tom Hastings, this book is really all because of Peace Voice and the need to speak to real people about peace and nonviolence . . . you may take credit for that and enjoy it to the utmost.

To all my Pace e Bene/Campaign Nonviolence friends, it was our years together seeking to build a culture of peace and active nonviolence that helped me to see how the war and violence culture steeps us all like frogs in boiling water unless we jump out. I've taken a leap, and hopefully this book can serve as an act of nonviolent intervention to help the next generation escape the hot waters of war.

My gratitude to the peace movement is not complete without honoring my father, Jim Cook, who stood tall in my eyes for being a conscientious objector and organizer against the Vietnam War. I would also like to thank my mother, Kathryn Simonds, for three things: countless hours of Irish-American storytelling around a large, family-packed table; 936 trips to the public library (once per week for every year of my childhood); and for insisting that I use nonviolent options for resolving my conflicts with my siblings. I'd also like to honor my grandfathers, Charles E. Cook and Charles A. Simonds, for each being impressive storytellers in their own ways.

This book would not be as enjoyable without the feedback and assistance of my early readers, Cindy Reinhardt, Jenny Bird, Veronica Pelicaric, and Marirose Nightsong. Additionally, thank you to Tom Hastings, Jaige Trudel, Michael Colvin, and many others for catching some of those pesky typos. Dariel Garner is the backbone of this whole story, spending countless hours asking questions of "what if" and "how about". Thank you from the bottom of my heart.

I want to commend all my Community Publishers for this book and previous book. You have consistently shown vision and faith in the process and importance of writing these stories. I am always deeply honored by our collaborative effort to publish these books.

Special thanks goes out to my numerous dance teachers and spiritual influences. Their efforts are woven into this story in profound ways. I would also like to acknowledge the beautiful Earth that has held us all through all of our work for peace, art, beauty, expression, knowledge, and change. Without her, we would have no ground to stand on as we bring this magic into being.

And lastly, thanks to the children for whom this book is truly written.

With love and gratitude,

Rivera Sun

Q & A with RIVERA SUN

· · · · ·

What inspired *Azar*, the Way Between?

The Way Between is inspired by a common phrase in the field of conflict studies: between fight and flight, there's a third option. That third option is nonviolent action, which is neither passivity nor violence. It confronts injustice and oppression without adding more violence, injustice, or oppression to the world. It's a powerful force, and people are increasingly using it to resolve socio-political problems around the globe. It is being used more often than violence, and is proving to be twice as effective as violence in achieving some major goals, such as overthrowing dictators, ending occupations, and expelling foreign invasions. The Way Between is a 21st century update to our love of fantasy stories. We've got better options than violence that still include all the courage, action, adventure, cleverness, and danger that humanity still seems to love in its stories.

Going further, there are really two aspects of your question: inner and outer *Azar*. Inner *Azar* is a blend of meditation, peace training, nonviolent conflict resolution, de-escalation skills, restorative justice, nonviolent struggle, truth and reconciliation, peacebuilding, and more.

271

Outer *Azar*, the physical form, is a blend from many sources. Aikido, of course, but also Capoeira, a Brazilian martial arts form. Capoeira was driven underground during the colonial period of Brazil's history and turned into a dance. In it, the two dancers whip around each other swiftly with flying arms and legs! The goal is to come close to striking without actually hitting one another. It's incredible. Another influence on *Azar* is modern dance, which I studied for many years.

Were you like Ari Ara as a child?
Great question! I have red hair and a temper. I even had a couple of sheep when I was younger. I love to move, mostly in dance. Unlike Ari Ara, I learned to read and write at a young age. I was also (believe it or not) incredibly shy when I was eleven. I had two loving parents who taught me a lot about peace, justice, and nonviolence. My mother taught me not to use violence. (That temper of mine was leading me into some not very nice behaviors toward my younger brothers.) My father was a peace activist and a conscientious objector. They were part of a generation of parents who debunked the myth of "spare the rod, spoil the child" and refused to spank any of their children. They found other options for resolving our household conflicts over chores or disputes. It was a formative upbringing, and one for which I am very grateful.

What's the backstory on the Fanten?
The Fanten were partly inspired by some research I did on Celtic sagas and legends. There were references to earlier races of people, some of which became demi-gods or the Faerie Folk as time went on. I imagine, however, that at the time of the sagas, they were much less vague and far more human. The Fanten are a culture hovering at the edge of another dominant

culture (the Marianans), maintaining their identity, but with some difficulties. As we look around our world today, I think we see this story playing out in many different cultures in thousands of different ways. As an activist, I've learned more about the indigenous peoples of North American and beyond. Several indigenous and activist friends have helped me see and better understand the issues around indigenous rights and the struggle to maintain one's culture over centuries of oppression and domination. Reflecting on these themes informed how I wrote about the Fanten's relationship with the Marianans. The two groups in the novel are not quite the same dynamic as indigenous and settler/colonist groups in our world. The fictional groups have historically cohabitated different regions. But, the Marianans tend to dominate their landscape and discriminate against all others groups. We'll be looking closely at this dynamic in the next book in the series. I think these are important subjects to explore if we are ever going to create a just and respectful world.

Have you ever trained in martial arts?

I have not. I trained in modern dance in college, and spent seven years running a professional dance theater company in central California. Just down the street from my house was an aikido studio. On warm days, they used to open the wide, shuttered doors and I could watch the practices from the end of my driveway. There was a fierce beauty to the movement that I admired, but I was busy training in dance at the time.

Is there a real life inspiration for the character of Minli?

When I was in college, I had a friend with a prosthetic leg. He was - and still is - an amazing musician. Every time we went to campus, we had to go up and over a huge hill to get there. I could never make it up all the way on my bike. My friend used to laugh at me because he - with his one leg! - could. I've never forgotten that, nor the lessons I've learned from people with different abilities than my own.

Why did you choose to make Ari Ara unable to read?

My mother learned to read in fourth grade. She had an amazing teacher, Eleanor P. Merrill, who connected with my mother. Like all great teachers (and Shulen in the novel), Mrs. Merrill knew that if she connected a challenging skill (reading) to something my mother enjoyed, she would be more likely to learn the difficult skill. Since my mother loved to draw, Mrs. Merril would combine reading lessons with drawing lessons. It worked! And, it demonstrated that people learn at different paces, times, and in different ways. I thought this is an important understanding for all of us, including children. By making the main character of this book struggle with reading, my hope is to uplift the idea that we all have gifts and strengths, as well as challenges and struggles.

Our culture puts a lot of emphasis on the importance of reading and writing and mathematics and science. There are many other kinds of knowledge and learning, however. In the book, Ari Ara has a "genius for movement". I've known dancers like that, or martial artists. Some people are incredible musicians or painters or cooks or carpenters. Others have amazing skills at healing or deep listening or mentoring. I think we can do better at celebrating the different kinds of intelligence and the different skills that humanity carries. We will be a richer and more balanced society if we do.

The other reason Ari Ara struggles to learn to read and write is because we often see highly talented people and assume that they are perfect and never have any challenges. However,

274

more often than not when people excel at one skill, they struggle at another. Understanding this helps us see ourselves in a similar light, and gives us the ability to both celebrate our strengths and acknowledge our weaknesses.

What about Shulen? Where did he come from?

I am honored to have many friends who are members of Veterans for Peace, an organization of men and women who have served in the US military who organize for and advocate peace. One thing they have taught me is the vast differences between the popular culture's mythologies about soldiers or warriors, and the realities they experienced in the military and at war. I have two friends, in particular, who have meant a lot to me, and I wanted to honor them with a character that brings up some of the perspectives, concerns, and issues that I have heard them discuss.

Are the Desert People a reference to our current conflicts in the Middle East?

Not directly, though there are many insights to be drawn from the parallels that do occur. The Desert People in this book are mainly understood through the lens of the Marianans . . . which isn't always accurate and is often very prejudiced. Many times in the book, Shulen challenges Ari Ara and others to look beyond their preconceptions or to withhold judgment until they are better informed. I feel that this is very true for our real world, wherever there is conflict. We often dehumanize our "enemies" as our nation prepares to launch wars. Conversely, the process of building peace often requires increasing understanding on both sides of a conflict. In another book in this series, we'll hear the Desert People's side of the story. Stay tuned.

Are the Stories of the Third Brother written down anywhere?

They should be! All of the stories mentioned in the novel are adaptations from real life stories. The tale of Alaren and the bandits is loosely based on Vinoba Bhave and JP Narayan and the Dacoits of India. The truth-telling is inspired by the Truth and Reconciliation processes that have been used in South Africa and other places. The story of the blacksmiths, of course, is straight out of the famous Biblical line in Isaiah: *they shall beat their swords into ploughshares and study war no more.* There are hundreds more. Adapting these real life examples into Stories of the Third Brother would be a wonderful writing project at some point.

In the book, followers of the Way Between were persecuted for promoting peace. Where did that idea come from?

During the Vietnam War, the Buddhist monk, Thich Nhat Hanh and his fellow practitioners of Engaged Buddhism, attempted to stop the war and provide humanitarian relief to all sides. They were killed by both sides, repressed, imprisoned, and exiled. However, their efforts played a very important role in building the peace movement's opposition to the war. There are many other examples of peace activists being persecuted for advocating peace and the end of wars. Henry David Thoreau, for example, was jailed for refusing to pay a war tax for a war he viewed as unjust; it is from this experience that the term "civil disobedience" came into being.

So, will there be a sequel?

Yes! Look for *The Lost Heir* in 2018-2019.

ABOUT THE AUTHOR

Rivera Sun is the author of *The Way Between, The Lost Heir, Billionaire Buddha, The Dandelion Insurrection* and *The Roots of Resistance,* as well as several other novels, a study guide to nonviolent action, three books of poetry, and numerous articles. She has red hair, a twin sister, and a fondness for esoteric mystics. She went to Bennington College to study writing as a Harcourt Scholar and graduated with a degree in dance. She lives in an earthship house in New Mexico, where she writes essays and novels. She is a nonviolence trainer and an activist. Rivera has been an aerial dancer, a bike messenger, and a gung-fu style tea server. Everything else about her - except her writing - is perfectly ordinary.

Rivera Sun also loves hearing from her readers.
Email: rivera@riverasun.com
Facebook: Rivera Sun
Twitter: @RiveraSunAuthor
Website: www.riverasun.com

If you enjoyed *The Way Between* . . .
you can help inspire others to the possibilities
of waging peace and active nonviolence
in the following ways:

Spread the word about the book.
Tell your friends.
Post about it on social media.
Review the book on your favorite online bookstore.
Recommend it to your book group.
Suggest it to teachers and students.

Thank you!

The Lost Heir: An Unruly Royal,
An Urchin Queen, and A Quest For Justice

Going beyond dragon-slayers and sword-swingers, *The Lost Heir* blends fantasy and adventure with social justice issues in an unstoppable story that will make you cheer!

Mariana Capital is in an uproar! A half-wild orphan has been discovered to be the long-lost daughter of the King of the Desert and the Queen of Mariana. As the heir to two thrones, Ari Ara is thrust into a world of nobles and street urchins, warriors and merchants, high fashion and dangerous plots. The splendor dazzles her until the day she sneaks out to explore the city and makes a shocking discovery . . . the luxury of the nobles is built on the forced labor of her father's people. With the help of an urchin queen, a monkish young scholar, a desert seamstress, and a mysterious hawk keeper, she sets out on a quest for justice. Before she knows it, she's sparked an uprising like nothing Mariana Capital has ever seen!

With all the fun of a sword-swinging adventure, but without the violence, *The Lost* Heir spins a spectacular story with strong female characters and powerful social justice themes. "Armed" with nonviolence and love, Ari Ara sets out to restore the honor and dignity of both her peoples. A shero with spunk and spark, Ari Ara confronts prejudice, discrimination, bullying, and injustice with all the action, adventure, magic, and fantasy that readers love!

Kids, parents, and teachers agree: you'll love this book!

A rare gem of a book, a must read, it charts the way forward in this time of turmoil and transformation." - Velcrow Ripper, director Occupy Love, Genie Award Winner

"When fear is used to control us, love is how we rebel!" Under a

gathering storm of tyranny, Zadie Byrd Gray whirls into the life of Charlie Rider and asks him to become the voice of the Dandelion Insurrection. With the rallying cry of life, liberty, and love, Zadie and Charlie fly across America leaving a wake of revolution in their path. Passion erupts. Danger abounds. The lives of millions hang by a thin thread of courage, but in the midst of the madness, the golden soul of humanity blossoms . . . and miracles start to unfold!

"This novel will not only make you want to change the world, it will remind you that you can." - Gayle Brandeis, author of *The Book of Dead Birds*, winner of the Bellwether Prize for Socially Engaged Fiction

"Close your eyes and imagine the force of the people and the power of love overcoming the force of greed and the love of power. Then read *The Dandelion Insurrection*. In a world where despair has deep roots, *The Dandelion Insurrection* bursts forth with joyful abandon." - Medea Benjamin, Co-founder of CodePink

"THE handbook for the coming revolution!" - Lo Daniels, Editor of Dandelion Salad

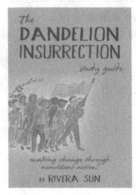

Praise for Rivera Sun's *Billionaire Buddha*

BILLIONAIRE BUDDHA

A NOVEL BY RIVERA SUN

From fabulous wealth to unlimited blessings, the price of enlightenment may bankrupt billionaire Dave Grant. Emotionally destitute in the prime of his career, he searches for love and collides with Joan Hathaway. The encounter rattles his soul and unravels his world. Capitalism, property, wealth, mansions: his notions of success crumble into dust. From toasting champagne on top of the world to swigging whiskey with bums in the gutter, Dave Grant's journey is an unforgettable ride that leaves you cheering!

". . . inspirational and transformational! An enjoyable read for one's heart and soul."
-Chuck Collins, senior scholar, Institute for Policy Studies; co-author with Bill Gates Sr. of 'Wealth and Our Commonwealth'

". . . inspiring a skeptic is no easy task and Rivera Sun manages to do so, gracefully, convincingly, and admirably."
- Casey Dorman, Editor-in-Chief, Lost Coast Review

"People, if you haven't gotten your copy of *Billionaire Buddha* yet, you are letting a rare opportunity slip through your fingers. It's that good."
- Burt Kempner, screenwriter, producer and author of children's books

"This is the kind of book that hits you in the gut and makes you stop and think about what you just read."
- Rob Garvey, reader

"A clear and conscious look at our times and the dire need for a real change to heart based living."
- Carol Ranellone, reader

CPSIA information can be obtained
at www.ICGtesting.com
Printed in the USA
LVHW032045020222
710071LV00001B/38